YESHUA,
the *Messiah,*
the God-Man

Carroll Roberson

WESTBOW
PRESS®
A DIVISION OF THOMAS NELSON
& ZONDERVAN

WestBow Press books may be ordered through booksellers or by contacting:

WestBow Press
A Division of Thomas Nelson & Zondervan
1663 Liberty Drive
Bloomington, IN 47403
www.westbowpress.com
1 (866) 928-1240

ISBN: 978-1-5127-0737-3 (sc)

Library of Congress Control Number: 2015912758

Print information available on the last page.

WestBow Press rev. date: 08/24/2015

INDEX

INTRODUCTION

When we read the words *"Lord Jesus Christ"*, sometimes we fail to understand the magnitude of those words. In the Hebrew tongue, they would be pronounced, *"Yeshua Ha Mashiach."* They are declaring that *Yeshua* was the *Lord* and that He was also the *Messiah*! The two titles of *Yeshua*, *"Lord"* and *"Christ"*, develop along two separate paths and have distinct theological implications. *Yeshua the Messiah* is referring to His title, the promised One, who had been foretold from about 1700-400BC. *Yeshua* as *"Lord,"* refers to His deity and to the God of the Old Testament.

The Hebrew word *"mashiach"* means *"anointed"*, and is used some 39 times in the Old Testament, sometimes when describing the anointed kings, like in **I Chron. 16:21-22**, or a priest, like in **Lev.4:3**, or someone who is to carry out God's purpose, such as Cyrus in **Isa.45:1**. It is used when referring to God's *mashiach* in **Psalm 2:2**. There are some 9 occurrences where the word describes the future anointed *One* in the line of David. The old rabbis referred to 456 separate OT passages that promised a coming Messiah. There are *direct* prophecies and then there are *typical* prophecies. However, the doctrine of the Messiah is not limited to just the name *mashiach*. Sometimes the Messiah is used in terms of the *son*, **Psalm 2:7**, *branch*, **Zech.6:12**, *servant*, **Isa.41-53**, and *king*, **Zech.9:9**.

Yeshua the Messiah, embodied the ideal Israel, fulfilling in His person what Israel as a people had failed to fulfill. Even though this is a broader study on the Messiahship of *Yeshua,* it is a fascinating study indeed. The dual roles of the Messiah, both his suffering and reigning, is the key to not only understanding the scriptures, but to understanding his role as it pertains to corporate Israel.

The Messiah had to be the ideal *prophet-priest-king.* We can see him as a *prophet* in **John 6:14, 7:40,** as a *priest* in **Hebrews 4:14, 10:11-12,** and as *king* in **Rev.19:16.** *Yeshua* is always the anointed *king,* even at his birth, but He rules and reigns as *king* during the Millennial Kingdom.

The Hebrew word *"mashiach"* was later translated into the Greek word, *"christos",* and later translated into the English word *"Christ".* This English word *"Christ"* is found 295 times in the New Testament, and the English name of *"Jesus Christ",* or *"Yeshua Mashiach"* is found 135 times in the New Testament. The English name reversed, *"Christ Jesus"* or *"Mashiach Yeshua"* is found 95 times in the New Testament. Other combinations include *"Christ the Lord"* or *"Messiah the Lord,"* in **Luke 2:11,** or *"the Lord's Christ,"* or *"the Lord's Messiah,"* in **Luke 2:26.**

The word *"Messiah"* is generally treated in the New Testament as synonymous with *Jesus of Nazareth. Yeshua* is not accepted by most religious Jews in the world today as the *Messiah.* They are still awaiting the first coming of their *Messiah,* while believing Jews and Gentiles are awaiting the Second Coming of the *Messiah.* Christians believe that the Old Testament mentions two comings of one *Messiah.* The followers of *Yeshua* in the first century were called *Christians* in **Acts 11:26,** because they believed *Yeshua* to be the *Messiah* of the old Hebrew scriptures.

When we turn in the New Testament we find phrases like *"Jesus, who is called Christ"*, in **Matthew 1:16**, and *"The beginning of the gospel of Jesus Christ, the Son of God,"* in **Mark 1:1.** We find that the primary purpose of John's gospel was so that people *"might believe that Jesus is the Christ, the Son of God; and that believing ye might have life through his name."* **John 20:31.** When we read in the New Testament epistles, we find words like *"in Christ"*, or *"in Messiah,"* in places like **I Cor.4:15**, and **Romans 12:5,** describing the position of the followers of *Yeshua.*

In the following pages I have tried, through the Lord's help, to reveal and hopefully unravel some unique but unusual truths about *Yeshua.* I pray that the history and the Old and New Testaments will unite together like the dew on top of Mt. Hermon, to make this book bring blessings to many and glory to the Most High. So as we embark on this fascinating study on the Messiahship of *Yeshua,* may we have ears to hear and eyes to see, that there is only *One* who could have possibly been the long awaited Messiah of Israel; and his name is *Yeshua*!

THE SEED OF THE WOMAN

One of the most perplexing chapters in the entire Bible is **Genesis 3**. But out of the darkness of that conversation between a serpent, a woman, and a man, we find the first promise of a coming Redeemer. This first announcement has been called the *"protevangelium,"* meaning, *"the first announcement of the good news of the gospel."*

"And I will put enmity between thee and the woman, and between thy seed and her seed; it shall bruise thy head, and thou shalt bruise his heel." **Gen.3:15.**

We find that this promised *seed of the woman* will suffer in the process of defeating Satan. Consider making the biblical connection to **Genesis 3:15** with prophecies like, *"he was wounded for our transgressions, he was bruised for our iniquities."* **Isa.53:5.** As well as, *"Yet it pleased the Lord to bruise him."* **Isa.53:10.**

There are four basic truths about this prophecy in Genesis that we can see woven throughout the rest of the sacred scriptures:

1. *Unique Birth* – The seed of a woman (**Isa.7:14**, Virgin born)
2. *A Male Seed* - His heel, (**Isa.9:6**, Child and son)

1

3. *Supernatural* – Defeat Satan, a supernatural being (The Mighty God, **Isa.9:6**)
4. *Human* – Born from a woman (**Isa.7:14, Luke 2:7**)

A battle would begin between the *seed of a woman* and the *seed of the serpent* throughout the history of Israel. Many times we fail to see that Satan has a *seed* as well, and we see that seed trying to destroy Israel in the Old Testament, in places like **Gen.15:13**, **Exo.1**, **Esther**, and even tried to kill the *seed of the woman* after He was born into the world, **Matt.2:16, Rev.12:1-6.**

When the Messiah came into the world, He would find that the *seed of the serpent* was even controlling the religious establishment of Israel, **John 8:44.** He would see the disease and defilement that Satan had brought into the world, **Luke 13:16, John 11:35.** The Messiah would promise everlasting life to everyone who would trust in him, **John 3:16.** God intended for man to live forever, and even after sin came into the world, Adam still lived to be 930 years of age, **Gen.5:1-5.** The *seed of the woman* would restore the death that the *seed of the serpent* had brought into the world.

So as we read this first prophecy, we must realize that this is only the beginning of Messianic prophecies throughout the scriptures. Israel's Messiah will descend from *Shem*, **Gen.9:26**, from *Abraham*, **Gen.12:3**, from *Isaac*, **Gen.26:3**, from *Jacob*, **Gen.35:11-12**, from *Judah*, **Gen.49:10**, from *David*, **2 Sam.7:12-16**, and from *Zerubbabel*, **Hag.2:23.** He will be born in *Bethlehem Ephrathah*, **Micah 5:2**, before the *temple* is destroyed, **Dan.9:24-26**, 70 AD. He will be called a *Nazarene*, **Isa.11:1, Matt.2:23**, and have his ministry in the land of the *shadow of death* (Zebulun and Naphtali, Galilee), **Isa.9:1-2, Matt.4:13-16.** The promised Messiah would be *rejected* by his own people, **Isa.53:3, John 1:11**, and would be a *light to the Gentiles,* **Isa.42:6, Luke 2:32**. During his first coming, the Messiah would suffer through the *death of a cross,* **Psalm 22, Zech.12:10, 13:6, Matthew 27**. His days would be *prolonged,* **Isa.53:10, Luke 24**, and He will be *caught up to heaven and the throne,* **Luke 24:50-53, Acts 1:9-11, Rev.12:5.**

NOAH AND HIS
THREE SONS

"And Noah began to be an husbandman, and he planted a vineyard: And he drank of the wine, and was drunken; and he was uncovered within his tent. And Ham, the father of Canaan, <u>saw the nakedness of his father, and told his two brethren without</u>. And Shem and Japheth took a garment, and laid it upon both their shoulders, and went backward, and covered the nakedness of their father: and their faces were backward, and they saw not their father's nakedness. And Noah awoke from his wine, and <u>knew what his younger son had done unto him</u>. And he said, <u>Cursed be Canaan</u>; a servant of servants shall he be unto his brethren. And he said, <u>Blessed be the Lord God of Shem</u>; and Canaan shall be his servant. God shall enlarge Japheth, and he shall dwell in the tents of Shem; and Canaan shall be his servant." Gen.9:20-27.

The phrases that I have underscored deserve special attention, because there is something that took place in this passage that sets the stage for a major part of the Messianic history. As a result of the supernatural fallen angels having intercourse with the daughters of men, and produced a wicked race of supernatural beings, called the *nephillim*, **Gen.6:1-4**, God sent the horrific judgment of the flood on the entire world. God sent a *"bow in the cloud"* as a sign that He would never perform that same kind of judgment again, **Gen.9:12-17**. It's very interesting to me that we also see a *rainbow* over the throne in heaven, in **Rev.4:3**, as another sign of God's mercy.

The deluge has now passed, the ark has rested, and a new world awaited Noah and his family. Noah's three sons; Shem, Ham, and Japheth, would be the progenitors of new life on the earth. We find a very interesting little piece of information in **Gen.9:18**, that says, *"Ham was the father of Canaan."* Then we find the sad story of Noah becoming drunk with wine. God records the victories and the failures of his greatest servants in the Bible. Not only was Noah drunk with wine, it is believed by many that Ham committed some kind of incest with his father. The term *"saw the nakedness of his father,"* occurs in the Torah about incest relationships, in **Lev.18:6-18**. Then to make matters even worse, Ham went out and *"told"* (Hebrew *nagad*, or *boasted*) it to his brethren, **Gen.9:22**. But Shem and Japheth did not share in the disgraceful act. They walked backward and covered the nakedness of Noah, their father. When Noah awoke, he realized what had happened. The scriptures record some profound prophecies that Noah uttered, one curse and two blessings. These prophecies would affect the entire human race, and that is why we need to look at them separately.

HAM- *"Cursed be Canaan; a servant of servants shall he be unto his brethren."* **Gen.9:25.**

Noah was dishonored by one of his sons, so Ham would be dishonored by one of his sons, Canaan. Canaan and his descendants would follow in the footsteps of their father, Ham. Ham's children, Cush, (Ethiopia) Mizraim, (Egypt) and Put, (North Africa, Libya) all settled in the territory of present day Africa. This does not mean that Africa is a cursed country and that African Americans need to be enslaved. The descendants of Canaan did not settle in Africa. The Canaanites proved to be a very ungodly and sensuous group of people. **Lev.18:3.** This is part of the historical backdrop to the passage concerning the incest laws. It's very interesting to see that Canaan's descendants would later settle in the *land of Canaan,* which was the land that God would later promise to Abraham, **Gen.12:5-7.** The Canaanites were slaves under Joshua, **Josh.9:23,** and later under Solomon, **I Kings 9:20-21,** thus fulfilling the prophetic curse of slavery on the Canaanites.

SHEM- *"Blessed be the Lord God of Shem: and Canaan shall be his servant."* **Gen.9:26.**

Noah now pronounces a spiritual blessing on Shem. Notice the blessing says, *"the Lord God of Shem."* In the Hebrew original, "the YHVH ELOHIM." The "YHVH," would later become known as *"Yehovah,"* which would also be part of the name of Israel's Messiah, *"Yahshua,"* or *"Yeshua."* So what this verse is actually saying is that Israel's long awaited Messiah, *"Yeshua,"* would be the *Lord* of Shem and his descendants. God's covenant would be with the <u>line of Shem</u>. From Genesis through Revelation, God deals almost exclusively with Shem and his descendants, such as: *Abraham, Isaac, Jacob, Judah, David,* and finally, *Yeshua, the Messiah!* (**Luke 3:23-26**, Notice the name Semei, a Shemite)

JAPHETH – *"God shall enlarge Japheth, and he shall dwell in the tents of Shem; and Canaan shall be his servant."* **Gen.9:27.**

The last of Noah's prophecies concerns Japheth and his descendants. Japheth's sons include, Gomer, Magog, Javan, and Meshech. These tribes would later settle in the regions of Europe and Russia. Just think about all of the cultures that came out of Europe and extends to this very day to the rest of the world? Noah said that Japheth's descendants would *"dwell in the tents of Shem."* In the middle east culture, to *dwell in the tents* of someone means to share in the belongings of the one who owns the tent.

(I recall several years ago when I was filming a TV program in Nazareth, Israel. After we had finished filming, the owner of the home, who owned the balcony from which we had filmed, expected me to enjoy coffee with he and his family. It was the custom for me to sit down and partake of his blessings. And even though I hated the coffee, I realized more of the culture in Israel that goes back thousands of years)

Someday the descendants of Japheth, who would be the Gentiles, would dwell in the tents of the Shemites. Gentiles would partake of the blessing that Noah pronounced upon Shem. Listen to the powerful words of *Yeshua the Messiah,* Shem's greatest son:

"And other sheep I have, which are not of this fold." **John 10:16.**

We see all of this played out in the book of Acts, where one of the descendants of Japheth, *Cornelius,* came to dwell in the tents of Shem. **Acts 10.** Because of God's mercy, even the descendants of Ham can be saved if they will believe in *Yeshua.* There is a beautiful picture of how the gospel relates to the descendants of each one of Noah's sons:

Acts 8- Conversion of the Ethiopian eunuch – Descendant of Ham

Acts 9 – Conversion of Saul – Descendant of Shem

Acts 10 – Conversion of Cornelius – Descendant of Japheth

THE SEED OF ABRAHAM

"And the Lord had said unto Abram, Get thee out of thy country, and from thy kindred, and from thy father's house, unto a land that I will shew thee: And I will make of thee a great nation, and I will bless thee, and make thy name great; and thou shalt be a blessing: And I will bless them that bless thee,, and curse him that curseth thee: and in thee shall all families of the earth be blessed." Gen.12:1-3

We must be clear, Abram was not a Hebrew, and he was not an Israelite, nor was he a Jew. Abram was a Syrian, **Deut.26:5**, who became a Hebrew in **Gen.14:13**. The name *"Hebrew,"* or *"Abar,"* means *"to pass over,"* and Abram passed over the Euphrates River into the land of Canaan. When Yahweh breathed upon Abram, his name became "Abraham," because the breath sound of *Yahweh* was placed in his name, and also because Abraham would become a father of a great nation. The first *"Israelite,"* was a man called *"Jacob,"* in **Gen.32:28**. Jacob's name would be part of the natural seed of the patriarch Abraham, but when God changed his name to *"Israel,"* it identified him with the spiritual part of the covenant that God had made with Abraham. We will look in the next chapter when the first time the name *"Jew,"* appears in scripture.

Out of all the covenants that are so important between God and Israel, the Abrahamic covenant is the foundation of the rest. This covenant involves a *people*, a *blessing*, and a *land*, and through *Yeshua the Messiah*, even the Gentiles are part of the spiritual blessings of this covenant, **Gal.3:6-9.** When studying the scriptures, it is crucial to make the connection between the Abrahamic covenant and *Yeshua.* The Jews and Arabs can claim a natural connection to Abraham, through Isaac and Ishmael, but only the believers in *Yeshua,* Jews or Gentiles, can make a claim to a spiritual part of the Abrahamic covenant.

"Christ hath redeemed us from the curse of the law, being made a curse for us: for it is written, Cursed is every one that hangeth on a tree: That the blessing of Abraham might come on the Gentiles through Jesus Christ; that we might receive the promise of the Spirit through faith." **Gal.3:13-14.**

"And if ye be Christ's, then are ye Abraham's seed, and heirs according to the promise." **Gal.3:29.**

Another most important part of the Abrahamic covenant is the land agreement. It was called Canaan, because the inhabitants were descendants of Canaan, the cursed grandson of Noah. Consider this verse:

"And I will give unto thee, and to thy seed after thee, the land wherein thou art a stranger, all the land of Canaan, for an everlasting possession; and I will be their God." **Gen.17:8.**

Even though Israel has never enjoyed all the land that God promised them, *(From the river of Egypt to the Euphrates River,)* that promise will be ultimately fulfilled when *Yeshua* the Messiah returns.

Abraham had no children, and yet, God told him that his seed would be as many as the stars in heaven. **Gen.15:5.** Then the scriptures tell us that Abraham believed God.

"And he believed in the Lord; and he counted it to him for righteousness." **Gen.15:6**.

This passage is so vitally important that the Apostle Paul and James quoted it in their epistles, some three different times. **Rom.4:3, Gal.3:6, James 2:23.**

God told Abraham that the covenant that He had made with him would be attacked, and Abraham's seed would even be enslaved.

"And he said to Abram, "Know of a surety that thy seed shall be a stranger in a land that is not theirs, and shall serve them; and they shall afflict them four hundred years." **Gen.15:13.**

God's covenant with Abraham would be fulfilled in spite of these attacks, and God would judge those people. God's covenant with Abraham would be unconditional, and nothing that Israel would do could invalidate this covenant.

THE TRIBE OF JUDAH

"Judah, thou art he whom thy brethren shall praise: thy hand shall be in the neck of thine enemies; thy father's children shall bow down before thee. Judah is a lion's whelp: from the prey, my son, thou art gone up: he stooped down, he couched as a lion, and as an old lion: who shall rouse him up? The sceptre shall not depart from Judah, nor a lawgiver from between his feet, until Shiloh come; and unto him shall the gathering of the people be." **Gen. 49:8-10**

The name *"Judah"* means, *"praise."* Judah would be the leader of his brothers and praised by his brothers. In the years following, it's interesting that as the tribes were marching through the wilderness, that it was the tribe of Judah that went first. **Numbers 10:14**. After Israel conquered the Promised Land, the first tribe to receive its allotment was Judah. **Joshua 15:1**. They were given the largest and most important sections of the land; which was the southern part with the largest population, including present-day Jerusalem. The tribe of Judah would later be used in the naming the Israelite people; the *"Judeans"* or simply, the *"Jews."*

Jacob's prophecy concerning Judah also included that he would be a conqueror. The blessing states that Judah's hand would be on the neck of his enemies, signifying that his enemies would be defeated. The greatest king in Old Testament history was King David, who was from the tribe of Judah. Notice the words that David placed in one of his songs in comparison to **Gen.49:8.**

"Thou hast also given me the necks of mine enemies; that I might destroy them that hate me." **Psalm 18:40.**

Because a lion is considered to be the king of beasts, Judah is compared to a *"lion."* This kingly motif is carried throughout the Old Testament and the New Testament. We know that *Yeshua* was from the tribe of Judah, and listen to these words from a scene in the throne room of heaven. **Rev.5:5-**

"And one of the elders saith unto me, Weep not: behold, the Lion of the tribe of Juda, the Root of David, hath prevailed to open the book, and to loose the seven seals."

In the dying blessing of Jacob, we see that the Messiah will come before *"the sceptre departs from Judah."* There are two possible dates as to when the sceptre departed Judah. The first date is 6AD, when the first Roman governor of Judaea, Coponius, took capital punishment out of the hands of Israel and placed it in the hands of Rome. The second possible date is 70AD, when the temple was destroyed in Jerusalem, by the Romans, and all of the written records of Jewish geneaology were destroyed. When we study **Luke 3,** Egyptian history, and Roman history, we believe the date of the birth of *Yeshua* the Messiah was the year 2BC, which happened before either of these two possible dates. *Yeshua* the Messiah came before the records were destroyed, and now, because there are no tribal records for anyone to find, nobody else can claim to be Israel's Messiah. Notice that we have a prophecy in the first book of the sacred scriptures that the Messiah will come through the *tribe of Judah*, and the announcement in the last book of the sacred scriptures that the Messiah is from the *tribe of Judah.*

This passage in Genesis also promises that the *"Shiloh"* will come. What is meant by the term *"Shiloh?"* It is the personal name of the King Messiah; the right of kingship; and the nations will submit to Him. From this moment on, the people looked for the Messiah to come through the *tribe of Judah.*

The gathering of the people unto the Messiah will be both believing Jews and Gentiles down through the centuries of time. Think of all of the saints from the Old Testament and the New Testament, and then think of all of the believers since the early first century, from all corners of the earth. The final gathering for the Jews will be when *Yeshua* the Messiah returns and they see the wounds in his hands. **Zechariah 12:10.**

THE RED HEIFER AND
THE MESSIAH

"And the Lord spake unto Moses and unto Aaron, saying, This is the ordinance of the law which the Lord hath commanded, saying, Speak unto the children of Israel, that they bring thee a red heifer without spot, wherein is no blemish, and upon which never came yoke." **Numbers 19:1-2.**

"For if the blood of bulls and of goats, and the ashes of an heifer sprinkling the unclean, sanctifieth to the purifying of the flesh: How much more shall the blood of Christ, who through the eternal Spirit offered himself without spot to God, purge your conscience from dead works to serve the living God?" **Hebrews 9:13-14.**

Without trying to just fill up a few pages with words, there has been a lot of media press about Jews trying to find a red heifer, or in Hebrew, a *parah adumah*, or hoping to find the ashes of a red heifer that were offered before the destruction of the temple in Jerusalem. Why? Because the unbelieving, religious Jews think that they have to find a red heifer before the sacrifices can begin in the new third temple. There has been an ongoing search in and around the Dead Sea for many years trying to find ashes from a red heifer that was sacrificed before 70AD. Without sounding disrespectful, this is an issue for the unbelieving Jews to resolve. Since they still live under the law, there is a reason why they

14

place so much emphasis on the red heifer. Let me give you a brief summary of **Numbers 19**.

Eleazar, the priest, led the red cow outside the camp, slaughtered it, and sprinkled some of its blood toward the Tabernacle seven times. The entire animal was then burned, and a mixture of cedar wood, hyssop, and scarlet material was cast onto the burning heap. The resulting ashes were kept in a clean place outside the camp. The purpose of the ashes was to ritually purify anyone who came in contact with a dead body. An unclean person had to be sprinkled with a mixture of the ashes with flowing water. Anyone who refused to go through this process was cut off from the assembly. This was such an unusual ritual that the one who actually did the sprinkling became unclean until the evening.

Now the writer of the New Testament book of Hebrews, *(some of the early church fathers say that it was Barnabas)* uses a Jewish style of teaching called, *kalvy'homer*, which compares the lesser with the greater. In other words, if the blood of a red heifer cleansed a person outwardly, then how much more does the blood of the Messiah cleanse a person inwardly? Notice the triune Godhead that is mentioned in **Heb.9:13-14**.

1) *Blood of the Messiah*
2) *Eternal Spirit*
3) *Living God*

While the efforts of sincere rabbis and dairymen make for interesting reading, they really miss God's intention. The red heifer's work was completed in *Yeshua* the Messiah, and will never be repeated. We are not looking for the ashes of a red cow, but we are looking for the second coming of Israel's Messiah, *Yeshua Ha Mashiach*!

MESSIAH THE STAR
AND SCEPTRE

"I shall see him, but not now: I shall behold him, but not nigh: there shall come a Star out of Jacob, and a Sceptre shall rise out of Israel, and shall smite the corners of Moab, and destroy all the children of Sheth." **Numbers 24:17.**

The perplexing prophecy of the Mesopotamian soothsayer, Balaam, has fascinated scholars for centuries. The Hebrew name comes from two words, *"bal,"* which means *"failure,"* and *"am,"* which means, *"people."* Balaam, was hired by Balak the king of Moab, to curse the people of Israel. Balaam accepted the challenge because he was motivated by greed and covetousness. There are three New Testament references to the wicked ways of Balaam, and all have a negative connotation: **2 Peter 2:15, Jude 11,** and **Rev.2:14**. The wicked way of Balaam is also mentioned in the Jewish Talmud: *"Those who have an evil eye, an arrogant spirit, and a greedy soul are among the disciples of the wicked Balaam. His disciples inherit Gehenna and descend into the well of destruction"* *(Abot 5:22)*

But when he came to curse the people of Israel, Balaam became only a channel through whom God would speak this great prophecy: *"And God put a word in the mouth of Balaam."* **Numbers 23:5.** God using a non-Israelite is unusual, but is also found in other places in the Bible. Other examples are Melchizedek, **Gen.14:18-20**, Jethro, **Ex.18:1**, and Cyrus, **Isa.44:28**.

Balaam found out that it was impossible to curse Israel, and that Israel cannot be destroyed. Even though Israel would waver in their faith and even drift off into worshipping false gods, the position of Israel was secure. Balaam found out that what God had told Abraham was true: *"I will bless them that bless thee, and curse him that curseth thee."* **Gen.12:1-3.** We are reminded of people who tried to curse Israel and it only turned out to be a blessing. The Egyptian ruler Pharaoh, the evil Persian ruler, Haman, the Syrian tyrant Antiochus Epiphanes, and when the evil German dictator Hitler tried to destroy Israel, the modern state of Israel was born.

There are several things about this strange prophecy that God spoke through Balaam that focuses on the future fulfillment of blessing on Israel that will come through their Messiah.

1) *Balaam saw an individual in the future*
2) *A Star*
3) *A Sceptre*
4) *He will destroy the Moabites*

The prophecy of the Messiah being *"A Star,"* connects to the story of the wise men at the birth of *Yeshua*, and also in the self-proclamation of *Yeshua* in the last chapter in Revelation.

"Now when Jesus was born in Bethlehem of Judaea in the days of Herod the king, behold, there came wise men from the east to Jerusalem, Saying, Where is he that is born King of the Jews? for we have seen his star in the east, and are come to worship him." **Matt.2:1-2.**

"I Jesus have sent mine angel to testify unto you these things in the churches. I am the root and the offspring of David, and the bright and morning star." **Rev.22:16.**

The other title that is prophesied through Balaam, is that the Messiah will be *"A Sceptre."* This tells us that the Messiah of Israel will be a King, a Ruler. Verses like these come to mind:

"The Lord said unto my Lord, Sit thou at my right hand, until I make thine enemies thy footstool. The Lord shall send the rod of thy strength out of Zion: rule thou in the midst of thine enemies." **Psalm 110:1-2.**

"Then shall the Lord go forth, and fight against those nations, as when he fought in the day of battle." **Zech.14:3.**

"And out of his mouth goeth a sharp sword, that with it he should smite the nations: and he shall rule them with a rod of iron." **Rev.19:15.**

The prophecy also talks about a future day when this Deliverer will smite the corners of Moab, *(Balak was king of Moab, who hired Balaam)* and destroy all the children of Sheth. This is not talking about the Messianic line that will come through Seth, but the future people who will call themselves *"the children of Sheth,"* but in reality they are unbelievers. Many Hebrew scholars think this prophecy is referring to a future time when the Messiah returns to destroy the Muslim nations that are bordering the land of Israel.

MESSIAH AND MOSES

"The Lord thy God will raise up unto thee a Prophet from the midst of thee, of thy brethren, like unto me; unto him ye shall hearken." **Deuteronomy 18:15.**

Moses was the meekest man upon the face of the earth, **Numbers 12:3**, and he was slow of speech, **Ex.4:10**, but Moses was so close to God that he was placed in the clift of the rock while God's glory passed by, **Ex.33:21**. No doubt, Moses was the greatest leader in the Old Testament. Moses chose to suffer with the people of God rather than enjoying the treasures of Egypt, **Heb.11:25-26**. He kept the very first Passover down in the land of Egypt to save the firstborn, **Exo.12:1-11**, and led the Israelites on dry ground at the parting of the Red Sea, **Exo.14**. Moses was a *redeemer* who brought God's people out of Egyptian bondage, but *Yeshua* the Messiah is the *Redeemer* who brings God's people out of the bondage of sin. Moses was a voice *from* God, while *Yeshua* was the voice *of* God. As great as Moses was, there was going to come *One* who would be greater, **Hebrews 3:1-6**. Moses represented the law and Elijah represented the prophets on the Mt. of Transfiguration in **Luke 9:27-36**, but *Yeshua* would fulfill the law and the prophets.

"And beginning at Moses and all the prophets, he expounded unto them in all the scriptures the things concerning himself." **Luke 24:27.**

God lays down the characteristics of this *Prophet* that is to come:

1) *Raised up by God (The Lord thy God will raise up)*
2) *An Israelite (from among you, from your brethren)*
3) *Like Moses (Like unto me)*
4) *He must be obeyed (Unto him ye shall hearken)*

This passage made such a deep impression on the Jews of the Old Testament and also on the Jews that settled back in Israel after the Babylonian captivity. Imbedded in the consciousness of the people was a conviction that a *Prophet* would someday arrive who would be greater than anyone who ever appeared in the history of Israel.

Listen to some of the verses in the New Testament where this expectation was so much on the hearts of the people:

"And he confessed, and denied not; but confessed, I am not the Christ. And they asked him, What then? Art thou Elias: And he saith, I am not. Art thou that prophet? And he answered, no." **John 1: 20-21 (Priests and Levites were questioning John the Baptist)**

"Then those men, when they had seen the miracle that Jesus did, said, This is of a truth that prophet that should come into the world." **John 6:14 (After Jesus fed the 5,000 at Galilee)**

"Many of the people therefore, when they heard this saying, said, Of a truth this is the Prophet." **John 7:40 (When Jesus was in Jerusalem)**

"For Moses truly said unto the fathers, A prophet shall the Lord your God raise up unto you of your brethren, like unto me; him shall ye hear in all things whatsoever he shall say unto you." **Acts 3:22 (In the sermon of Simon Peter at Pentecost)**

"This is that Moses, which said unto the children of Israel, A prophet shall the Lord your God raise up unto you of your brethren, like unto me; him shall ye hear." **Acts 7:37 (In the sermon of Stephen)**

The scribes and Pharisees who were ruling over the religious matters of the people during the time when *Yeshua* walked this earth, piously boasted that they believed the words of Moses. Listen to what *Yeshua* said:

"For had ye believed Moses, ye would have believed me: for he wrote of me." **John 5:46.**

One of *Yeshua's* disciples, Philip, knew that *Yeshua* was the one Moses wrote about.

"Philip findeth Nathanael, and saith unto him, We have found him, of whom Moses in the law, and the prophets, did write, Jesus of Nazareth, the son of Joseph." **John 1:45.**

God gave Moses a temporary covenant, but *Yeshua* the Messiah would bring in the everlasting covenant through His own blood.

"Behold, the days come, saith the Lord, that I will make a new covenant with the house of Israel, and with the house of Judah: Not according to the covenant that I made with their fathers in the day that I took them by the hand to bring them out of the land of Egypt; which my covenant they brake, although I was an husband unto them, saith the Lord: But this shall be the covenant that I will make with the house of Israel; After those days, saith the Lord, I will put my law in their inward parts, and write it in their hearts; and will be their God, and they shall be my people." **Jeremiah 31:31-33.**

"For this is my blood of the new testament, which is shed for many for the remission of sins." **Matthew 26:28.**

Moses was the mediator between the people of Israel and the God of Israel, but he disobeyed God and was not allowed to go into the promise land. *Yeshua* the Messiah is the true mediator between His people and God, and He was obedient in all things.

"For there is one God, and one mediator between God and men, the man Christ Jesus." **I Tim.2:5.**

No one can be justified by the deeds of the law, **Rom.3:20**, and the law was given through Moses, but salvation comes through *Yeshua* the Messiah.

"For the law was given by Moses, but grace and truth came by Jesus Christ." **John 1:17.**

MESSIAH IN THE
BOOK OF RUTH

"And Naomi took the child, and laid it in her bosom, and became nurse unto it. And the women her neighbours gave it a name, saying, There is a son born to Naomi; and they called his name Obed: he is the father of Jesse, the father of David. Now these are the generations of Pharez: Pharez begat Hezron, And Hezron begat Ram, and Ram begat Amminadab, and Amminadab begat Nahshon, and Nahshon begat Salmon, And salmon begat Boaz, and Boaz begat Obed, and Obed begat Jesse, and Jesse begat David." **Ruth 4:16-22.**

After the unhappy endings in the book of Judges we find this beautiful story that contains four chapters that starts with tragedy but has a happy ending. With a famine in the land of Bethlehem, Elimelech takes his wife Naomi, and their two sons, Mahlon and Chilion, to the land of Moab. While they were in the land of Moab, Elimelech died, and left Naomi with her two sons. Over a period of about ten years, the two sons married Moabite women; Orpah and Ruth, but the two sons died, leaving Naomi with her two daughter-in-laws. And one of the most moving parts of the story is that when Naomi heard that the famine was over in Bethlehem, she decided to return home, and she told both of her daughter-in-laws to stay in Moab. Orpah decided to stay in Moab and worship her gods, but Ruth made the decision to go back to Bethlehem, which was a strange land for Ruth, and live with Naomi. In so doing, Ruth made this vow:

"Intreat me not to leave thee, or to return from following after thee: for whither thou goest, I will go; and where thou lodgest, I will lodge: thy people shall be my people, and thy God, my God." **Ruth 1:16.**

This is the turning point of the story, where Ruth says that the people of Israel will be her new family, and her God will be the God of Israel! Wow! Naomi had a kinsman of her husband, named Boaz, who was a mighty man of wealth. While Ruth worked in the fields of Boaz, Boaz obeyed the God of Israel's laws, and took care of the stranger:

"Boaz commanded his young men, saying, Let her glean even among the sheaves, and reproach her not: And let fall also some of the handfuls of purpose for her, and leave them, that she may glean them, and rebuke her not." **Ruth 2:15-16.**

This entire setting was during the Feast of Shavuot (Pentecost) down in the land of Bethlehem. Because Boaz obeyed God, and did what was written in the law, **Lev.23:22, Deut.15:11,** God provided him a new wife, and even though she was a Moabitess, Ruth bare him a son. What a wonderful book! This is why the book of Ruth is read every year in Israel, among the religious Jews, during the Feast of Pentecost.

Most of the time we are so caught up in the characters of Elimelech, Naomi, Ruth, and Boaz; that we read fast over the last verses. But these last few verses hold the treasure of the book of Ruth.

Boaz was a descendant of the tribe of Judah, **Gen.49:10**, the tribe that would provide the coming Messiah. Boaz was also the son of the Canaanite Rahab, who believed in the God of Israel, **Joshua 2:9-11**, and Ruth would become the great-grandmother of David, the ancestor of the Messiah of Israel. God used a Moabitess, named Ruth, in keeping the Messianic bloodline from being stamped out by Satan. In **Deut.23:3-4**, a Moabite was excluded from the congregation of Israel for ten generations, because they did not provide bread and water for the children of Israel on their journeys, and also because they hired Balaam to try and curse Israel. God used another Gentile woman in the Messianic bloodline, among others are; Tamar, Rahab, and Bathsheba.

Their son, Obed would have a son named Jesse, **I Sam.16:1, Isa.11:1**, who would be the father of king David, whose lineage would produce *Yeshua* the Messiah. This particular part of the geneaology of the Messiah of Israel is such an important part of the sacred scriptures that it is echoed again in **Matthew 1:5-6**:

"And Salmon begat Booz of Rachab; and Booz begat Obed of Ruth; and Obed begat Jesse; and Jesse begat David the king."

MESSIAH THE SON
OF DAVID

"And it shall come to pass, when thy days be expired that thou must go to be with thy fathers, that I will raise up thy seed after thee, which shall be of thy sons; and I will establish his kingdom. He shall build me an house, and I will establish his throne for ever." I Chron.17:11-12, 2 Samuel 7:12-16.

David is considered to be the greatest king in the history of Israel. Even though David made sinful mistakes, his reign was the most brilliant. He united the tribes of Israel into one nation, and the will of God became the law of Israel. David secured undisputed possession of the country for Israel and his entire government was based upon religious principles. There is more space given in the Old Testament to the life of David than any other person. His descendants under patriarchal order were entitled to the throne. In the last words of David, the sweet psalmist of Israel, He mentions this everlasting covenant that God had made with him. **2 Sam.23:5.** This Davidic covenant would be *everlasting*, and not like the covenant that God made with Moses.

This covenant is mentioned several times in the Psalms. Here are a few of them:

"I have made a covenant with my chosen, I have sworn unto David my servant. Thy seed will I establish for ever, and build up thy throne to all generations. Selah." **Psalm 89:3-4.**

"Once I have sworn by my holiness that I will not lie unto David. His seed shall endure for ever, and his throne as the sun before me. It shall be established for ever as the moon, and as a faithful witness in heaven. Selah." **Psalm 89:35-37.**

"The Lord hath sworn in truth unto David; he will not turn from it; Of the fruit of thy body will I set upon thy throne." **Psalm 132:11.**

"The Lord said unto my Lord, Sit thou at my right hand, until I make thine enemies thy footstool." **Psalm 110:1. (Jesus used this passage to condemn the religious leaders of His day, by stating that the Messiah was more than a physical son of David, He was the Lord, Matt.22:41-46, Mark 12:35-37, Luke 20:41-44)**

One of the titles for the Messiah in the Old Testament is *"Branch,"* and two of the major prophecies that are written in the prophets that connect *Yeshua* with David are:

"And there shall come forth a rod out of the stem of Jesse (David's father), and a Branch **(Hebrew *"netzer"* = a descendant, figuratively speaking)** *shall grow out of his roots."* **Isa.11:1. (*Yeshua* grew up in Nazareth, Hebrew "Noztri" which was called the "Branch village", because after the Babylonian captivity, a small group of people settled there from the house and lineage of David. Notice the "word pun" and the similarity between "netzer"**

and "noztri". To this day the Hebrew word for "Christian" is "Noztri", because the first followers of *Yeshua* were called "people of the Nazarene")

"Behold, the days come, saith the Lord, that I will raise unto David a righteous Branch, **(Hebrew *"tsemach"*= sprout or bear, literally speaking)** *and a King shall reign and prosper, and shall execute judgment and justice in the earth."* **Jere.23:5.**

The very first words of the New Testament seem to lay down how important the covenants that God made with David and Abraham were to the first century Jewish believers in *Yeshua*.

"The book of the generation of Jesus Christ, the son of David, the son of Abraham." **Matt.1:1.**

Seventeen verses in the New Testament describe *Yeshua* the Messiah as the *"Son of David."* But how could *Yeshua* be the Son of David if David lived 1,000 years before *Yeshua*? Because of *Yeshua's* dual natures, being God and Man, His physical birth was through the house of David and His spiritual birth was through the Holy Spirit. Therefore, *Yeshua* could be called both the *"Son of David,"* and the *"Son of the Highest."*

"He shall be great, and shall be called the Son of the Highest: and the Lord God shall give unto him the throne of his father David." **Luke 1:32.**

Yeshua is a descendant of David through the adoption of Joseph and the virgin birth of Mary. Joseph and Mary were both from the house and lineage of David. **Luke 2:4.**

During the earthly ministry of *Yeshua*, notice how the Messianic title "Son of David," is included in the some of His miracles:

"And, behold, a woman of Canaan came out of the same coasts, and cried unto him, saying, Have mercy on me, O Lord, thou son of David; my daughter is grievously vexed with a devil." **Matt.15:22.**

"And when he heard that it was Jesus of Nazareth, he began to cry out, and say, Jesus, thou Son of David, have mercy on me. And many charged him that he should hold his peace: but he cried the more a great deal, Thou Son of David, have mercy on me." **Mark 10:47-48**

During the triumphal entry into Jerusalem, notice the title that the multitudes cried out to *Yeshua*:

"And the multitudes that went before, and that followed, cried, saying, Hosanna to the son of David: Blessed is he that cometh in the name of the Lord: Hosanna in the highest." **Matt.21:9.**

After the disciples spent 40 days with the risen *Yeshua*, and after *Yeshua* taught them who He was from the Old Testament, listen to part of the sermon that Simon Peter gave during the Feast of Pentecost:

"For David speaketh concerning him, I foresaw the Lord always before my face, for he is on my right hand, that I should not be moved: Therefore did my heart rejoice, and my tongue was glad; moreover also my flesh shall rest in hope: Because thou wilt not leave my soul in hell, neither wilt thou suffer thine Holy One to see corruption. Thou hast made known unto me the ways of life; thou shalt make me full of joy with thy countenance. Men and brethren, let me freely speak unto you of the patriarch David, that he is both dead and buried, and his sepulchre is with us unto this day. Therefore being a prophet,

and knowing that God had sworn with an oath unto him, that of the fruit of his loins, according to the flesh, he would raise up Christ to sit on his throne; He seeing this before spake of the resurrection of Christ, that his soul was not left in hell, neither his flesh did see corruption." **Acts 2:25-31.**

Even though the apostle Paul was called to take the gospel to the Gentiles, when he went into the Jewish synagogues, he reminded them of *Yeshua* coming from the house of David. Why? Because this was a promise that God made unto David, and it had to be fulfilled.

"And when he had removed him, (Saul) he raised up unto them David to be their king; to whom also he gave testimony, and said, I have found David the son of Jesse, a man after mine own heart, which shall fulfill all my will. Of this man's seed hath God according to his promise raised unto Israel a Saviour, Jesus." **Acts 13:22-23.**

When Paul was writing to the Gentile believers in Rome, notice these words:

"Concerning his Son Jesus Christ our Lord, which was made of the seed of David according to the flesh; And declared to be the Son of God with power, according to the spirit of holiness, by the resurrection from the dead." **Romans 1:3-4.**

Yeshua reminds us of the importance of the covenant that was given unto David just before the sacred scriptures are closed:

"I Jesus have sent mine angel to testify unto you these things in the churches. I am the root and the offspring of David, and the bright and morning star." **Rev.22:17.**

We must remember that the reason all of this has been recorded and preserved in the sacred scriptures is to show that *Yeshua* had to be the Messiah! At the time of *Yeshua's* birth into the world, Rome did not recognize the rights of the royal Davidic family, but one day when Yeshua returns, all of creation will recognize that *Yeshua* is the royal King of David, and He will sit on the throne in Jerusalem.

MESSIAH IN THE PSALMS

When I began to do an in-depth study on the Messiah in the writings of the Psalms, I was blown away with how many verses connect to the person of *Yeshua*. He quoted scriptures from the Psalms more than any other Old Testament book. One could write an entire volume on the Messiah in the Psalms. What makes the Psalms so rich is that when studying the Hebrew language, the original language of the Psalms, sometimes a verse will have a three dimensional message:

1) *The historical context*
2) *A future prophecy of the first or second coming of the Messiah*
3) *A personal application.*

Also, in Hebrew thought, a phrase from one verse can be tied together with a phrase from another verse, or one phrase out of one verse can be used to speak of a future fulfillment in the life of the Messiah. It is called *"a string of pearls."* When I study the Psalms I am reminded of what our Lord *Yeshua* said after His resurrection:

"And he said unto them, These are the words which I spake unto you, while I was yet with you, that all things must be fulfilled, which were written in the law of Moses, and in the prophets, and in the <u>psalms</u>, concerning me." **Luke 24:44.**

As our Lord taught His disciples from the Old Testament, He used the three sections of scripture that were used in the Hebraic style of teaching in the early first century; starting with the Torah, the Prophets, and the Psalms. The Hebrew scripture, or what we call the Old Testament, was believed to have been inspired in that order; and try to imagine hearing the emotions and the excitement in the voice of *Yeshua* when He explained who He was from the Psalms. In one sense, they all speak about Him in one way or the other, but because of time and space, I have selected some of the clearest Psalms that speak of the coming Messiah, with their fulfillment verses listed as well.

MESSIAH REJECTED BY JEWS AND GENTILE RULERS

"Why do the heathen rage, and the people imagine a vain thing? The kings of the earth set themselves, and the rulers take counsel together, against the Lord, and against his anointed." **Psalms 2: 1-2 = Acts 4:25-28.**

MESSIAH WOULD BE KING

"Yet have I set my king upon my holy hill of Zion." **Psalm 2:6 = John 12:12-13.**

MESSIAH WOULD BE THE SON OF GOD

"I will declare the decree: the Lord hath said unto me, Thou art my Son; this day have I begotten thee." **Psalm 2:7 = Luke 1:31-35.**

"Kiss the Son, lest he be angry, and ye perish from the way, when his wrath is kindled but a little. Blessed are they that put their trust in him." **Psalm 2:12 = John 3:36.**

MESSIAH WOULD BE PRAISED BY INFANTS

"Out of the mouth of babes and sucklings hast thou ordained strength because of thine enemies, that thou mightiest still the enemy and the avenger." **Psalm 8:2 = Matt.21:15-16**

MESSIAH WOULD BE GIVEN AUTHORITY OVER ALL THINGS

"Thou madest him to have dominion over the works of thy hands; thou hast put all things under his feet." **Psalm 8:6 = Matt.28:18, I Cor.15:24-25.**

MESSIAH WOULD BE RESURRECTED

"Therefore my heart is glad, and my glory rejoiceth: my flesh also shall rest in hope. For thou wilt not leave my soul in hell; neither wilt thou suffer thine Holy One to see corruption." **Psalm 16:8-10 = Matt.28:6, Acts 2:26-27.**

MESSIAH WOULD CRY OUT TO GOD

"My God, my God, why hast thou forsaken me?" **Psalm 22:1 = Matt.27:46.**

MESSIAH WOULD BE DESPISED

"But I am a worm, and no man; a reproach of men, and despised of the people." **Psalm 22:6 = Luke 23:21-23.**

MESSIAH WOULD BE MOCKED BY PEOPLE SHAKING THEIR HEADS

"All they that see me laugh me to scorn: they shoot out the lip, they shake the head." **Psalm 22:7 = Matt.27:39.**

MESSIAH WOULD BE MOCKED FOR TRUSTING GOD

"He trusted on the Lord that he would deliver him: let him deliver him, seeing he delighted in him." **Psalm 22:8 = Matt.27:41-43.**

MESSIAH WOULD BE AWARE OF THE FATHER FROM HIS YOUTH

"But thou art he that took me out of the womb: thou didst make me hope when I was upon my mother's breast." **Psalm 22:9 = Luke 2:40.**

MESSIAH WOULD BE CALLED FROM THE MOTHERS' WOMB

"I was cast upon thee from the womb: thou art my God from my mother's belly." **Psalm 22:10 = Luke 1:30-33.**

MESSIAH WOULD BE CRUCIFIED AND POURED OUT LIKE WATER

"I am poured out like water, and all my bones are out of joint: my heart is like wax; it is melted in the midst of my bowels." **Psalm 22:14 = John 19:34.**

MESSIAH WOULD THIRST

"My strength is dried up like a potsherd; and my tongue cleaveth to my jaws; and thou hast brought me into the dust of death." **Psalm 22:15 = John 19:28.**

MESSIAH WOULD BE SURROUNDED BY GENTILES AND JEWS AT THE CRUCIFIXION

"For dogs **(Gentiles)** *have compassed me: the assembly of the wicked* **(Jews)** *have inclosed me."* **Psalm 22:16a = Luke 23:36, Matt.27:41-43.**

MESSIAH'S HANDS AND FEET WOULD BE PIERCED

"they pierced my hands and feet." **Psalm 22:16b = Matt.27:38.**

MESSIAH'S GARMENTS WOULD BE DIVIDED

"They part my garments among them." **Psalm 22:18a = John 19:23-24.**

MESSIAH'S GARMENTS WOULD BE GAMBLED OVER

"and cast lots upon my vesture." **Psalm 22:18b = John 19:23-24.**

MESSIAH'S ATONEMENT WOULD ENABLE BELIEVERS TO BE HIS BRETHREN

"I will declare thy name unto my brethren: in the midst of the congregation will I praise thee." **Psalm 22:22 = Hebrews 2:10-12.**

MESSIAH'S BONES WILL NOT BE BROKEN

"He keepeth all his bones: not one of them is broken." **Psalm 34:20 = John 19:32-33.**

MESSIAH'S SACRIFICE WOULD REPLACE ALL SACRIFICES

"Sacrifice and offering thou didst not desire; mine ears hast thou opened: burnt offering and sin offering hast thou not required." **Psalm 40:6 = Hebrews 10:5-8.**

MESSIAH WOULD SAY THAT THE SCRIPTURES WERE WRITTEN OF HIM

"Then said I, Lo, I come: in the volume of the book it is written of me." **Psalm 40:7 = John 5:39, Luke 24:44, Hebrews 10:7.**

MESSIAH WOULD COME TO DO THE FATHER'S WILL

"I delight to do thy will, O my God: yea, thy law is within my heart." **Psalm 40:8 = John 5:30.**

MESSIAH'S BETRAYER WOULD BE A FRIEND WHO BROKE BREAD WITH HIM

"Yea, mine own familiar friend, in whom I trusted, which did eat of my bread, hath lifted up his heel against me." **Psalm 41:9 = Mark 14:17-18.**

MESSIAH BE GOD OF VERY GOD

"Thou lovest righteousness, and hatest wickedness: therefore God, thy God, hath anointed thee with the oil of gladness above thy fellows." **Psalm 45:7 = Hebrews 1:8-9.**

MESSIAH WOULD ASCEND BACK TO HEAVEN

"Thou hast ascended on high, thou hast led captivity captive: thou hast received gifts for men." **Psalm 68:18 = Matt.10:1, Luke 24:51.**

MESSIAH WOULD BE HATED WITHOUT A CAUSE

"They that hate me without a cause are more than the hairs of mine head." **Psalm 69:4 = Luke 23:13-22.**

MESSIAH WOULD BE REJECTED BY JEWS AND FAMILY

"I am become a stranger unto my brethren, and an alien unto my mother's children." **Psalm 69:8 = John 1:11, John 7:3-5.**

MESSIAH WOULD BE ANGERED BY DISRESPECT TOWARD THE TEMPLE

"For the zeal of thine house hath eaten me up." **Psalm 69:9 = John 2:13-17.**

MESSIAH WOULD BE OFFERED GALL AND VINEGAR

"They gave me also gall for my meat; and in my thirst they gave me vinegar to drink." **Psalm 69:21 = Matt.27:34.**

MESSIAH WOULD SPEAK IN PARABLES

"I will open my mouth in a parable: I will utter dark sayings of old."
Psalm 78:2 = Matt.13:34-35.

MESSIAH WOULD BE GOD'S FIRSTBORN

"Also I will make him my firstborn, higher than the kings of the earth."
Psalm 89:27 = Colossians 1:15.

MESSIAH WOULD BE THE ETERNAL CREATOR

"Of old hast thou laid the foundation of the earth: and the heavens are the work of thy hands. They shall perish, but thou shalt endure: yea, all of them shall wax old like a garment; as a vesture shalt thou change them, and they shall be changed: But thou art the same, and thy years shall have no end." **Psalm 102:25-27 = John 1:3, Colossians 1:17.**

MESSIAH WOULD BE ACCUSED BY FALSE WITNESSES

"For the mouth of the wicked and the mouth of the deceitful are opened against me: they have spoken against me with a lying tongue."
Psalm 109:2 = John 18:29-30.

MESSIAH'S BETRAYER WOULD HAVE A SHORT LIFE AND BE REPLACED

"Let his days be few; and let another take his office." **Psalm 109:8 = Acts 1:16-26**

MESSIAH WOULD BE CALLED LORD

"The Lord said unto my Lord, Sit thou at my right hand, until I make thine enemies thy footstool." **Psalm 110:1 = Matt.22:41-45.**

MESSIAH WOULD BE A PRIEST IN THE ORDER OF MELCHIZEDEK

"Thou art a priest for ever after the order of Melchizedek." **Psalm 110:4 = Hebrews 6:17-20.**

MESSIAH WOULD BE THE STONE REJECTED BY THE JEWS

"The stone which the builders refused is become the head stone of the corner." **Psalm 118:22 = Matt.21:42-43.**

MESSIAH WOULD COME IN THE NAME OF THE LORD

"Blessed be he that cometh in the name of the Lord." **Psalm 118:26 = Matthew 21:9, Matt.23:39.**

MESSIAH WOULD BE AT THE RIGHT HAND OF GOD

"The Lord at thy right hand shall strike through kings in the day of wrath." **Psalm 110:5 = Acts 7:56, I Peter 3:22.**

MESSIAH IN ISAIAH
(760-698BC ?)

Yeshua quoted from the book of Isaiah at least eight different times, or at least that what we have recorded in the gospel accounts. The reason for this is because the book of Isaiah is filled with prophecies about every part of the ministry of Israel's Messiah. Even the name *"Isaiah,"* is pronounced, *"Yeshayahuw,"* in Hebrew, which means, *"Yah has saved."* Isaiah was the first of the major prophets of Israel, during the 8th century BC. He prophesied for 64 years, during the reigns of Uzziah, Jotham, Ahaz, and Hezekiah. For many years of my ministry, I was guilty of underestimating the power and the magnitude of the writings of the Prophets of old. Listen to what the scriptures say:

"Surely the Lord God will do nothing, but he revealeth his secret unto his servants the prophets." **Amos 3:7.**

We should not be surprised when we read about so many prophecies in the writings of the Prophets that were fulfilled in the New Testament. God revealed to the Prophets a message to Israel of old, as well as, the prophecies of the future coming of Israel's Deliverer. Again, we find the deeper meanings of scripture when we study them from the original Jewish perspective. The verses are too numerous to mention, but here is a brief summary of many of the prophecies and fulfillments that connect us to *Yeshua* the Messiah from the book of Isaiah.

ISAIAH SAW YESHUA IN HIS GLORY

"Then said I, Woe is me! for I am undone; because I am a man of unclean lips, and I dwell in the midst of a people of unclean lips: for mine eyes have seen the King, the Lord of hosts." **Isa.6:5 = John 12:41.**

ISAIAH'S WORDS WOULD NOT BE RECEIVED, AND WAS ALSO FULFILLED IN THE EARTHLY MINISTRY OF YESHUA

"Make the heart of this people fat, and make their ears heavy, and shut their eyes; lest they see with their eyes, and hear with their ears, and understand with their heart, and convert, and be healed." **Isa.6:10 = Matt.13:13-15.**

ISAIAH WROTE ABOUT HOW THE MESSIAH WOULD BE BORN

"Therefore the Lord himself shall give you a sign; Behold, a virgin shall conceive, and bear a son, and shall call his name Immanuel." **Isa.7:14 = Matt.1:22-23.**

ISAIAH WROTE ABOUT WHERE THE MESSIAH'S EARTHLY MINISTRY WOULD BE HEADQUARTERED

"Nevertheless the dimness shall not be such as was in her vexation, when at the first he lightly afflicted the land of Zebulun and the land of Naphtali, and afterward did more grievously afflict her by the way of the sea, beyond Jordan, in Galilee of the nations. The people that

walked in darkness have seen a great light: they that dwell in the land of the shadow of death, upon them hath the light shined." **Isa.9:1-2 = Matt.4:13-16.**

ISAIAH WROTE ABOUT WHO THE MESSIAH WOULD BE

"For unto us a child is born, unto us a son is given: and the government shall be upon his shoulder: and his name shall be called Wonderful, Counsellor, The mighty God, The everlasting Father, The Prince of Peace." **Isa.9:6 = John 1:1-3, John 10:30, John 14:9.**

ISAIAH WROTE ABOUT THE MESSIAH BEING AN HEIR TO THE THRONE OF DAVID

"Of the increase of his government and peace there shall be no end, upon the throne of David, and upon his kingdom, to order it, and to establish it with judgment and with justice from henceforth even for ever." **Isa.9:7 = Luke 1:32-33, Matt.19:28.**

ISAIAH WROTE ABOUT THE ANCESTRY OF THE MESSIAH

"And there shall come forth a rod out of the stem of Jesse, and a Branch shall grow out of his roots." **Isa.11:1 = Matt.1:1, Matt.2:23.**

ISAIAH WROTE ABOUT THE MESSIANIC KINGDOM OF THE MESSIAH

"They shall not hurt nor destroy in all my holy mountain: for the earth shall be full of the knowledge of the Lord, as the waters cover the sea." **Isa.11:9 = Matt.26:29, Acts 1:6, Rev.20:6.**

ISAIAH WROTE ABOUT THE MESSIAH'S FORERUNNER

"The voice of him that crieth in the wilderness, Prepare ye the way of the Lord, make straight in the desert a highway for our God." **Isa.40:3 = Matt.3:3, John 1:23.**

ISAIAH WROTE ABOUT THE MESSIAH GOING TO THE GENTILES

"I the Lord have called thee in righteousness, and will hold thine hand, and will keep thee, and give thee for a covenant of the people, for a light of the Gentiles." **Isa.42:6 = Luke 2:32, Acts 13:47.**

ISAIAH WROTE ABOUT THE MODESTY AND MERCY OF THE MESSIAH

"He shall not cry, nor lift up, nor cause his voice to be heard in the street. A bruised reed shall he not break, and the smoking flax shall he not quench." **Isa.42:2-3 = Matt.12:19-20. (Bruised reeds and smoking flaxes were the people who society had thrown away who would receive mercy from the Messiah)**

ISAIAH WROTE ABOUT THE MESSIAH BEING THE FIRST AND THE LAST

"I the Lord, the first and with the last; I am he." **Isa.41:4.**

"Hearken unto me, O Jacob and Israel, my called; I am he; I am the first, I also am the last." **Isa.48:12 = Rev.1:11,17.**

ISAIAH WROTE ABOUT THE MESSIAH BEING SPIT UPON

"I gave my back to the smiters, and my cheeks to them that plucked off the hair: I hid not my face from shame and spitting." **Isa.50:6 = Matt.26:67.**

ISAIAH WROTE ABOUT THE MESSIAH BEING DISFIGURED THROUGH SUFFERING

"As many were astonied at thee; his visage was so marred more than any man, and his form more than the sons of men." **Isa.52:14.**

"For he shall grow up before him as a tender plant, and as a root out of a dry ground: he hath no form nor comeliness; and when we shall see him, there is no beauty that we should desire him." **Isa.53:2 = Mark 15:15-19.**

ISAIAH WROTE ABOUT THE BLOOD OF THE MESSIAH MAKING AN ATONEMENT FOR SIN

"But he was wounded for our transgressions, he was bruised for our iniquities: the chastisement of our peace was upon him; and with his stripes we are healed." **Isa.53:5 = I Peter 1:24.**

ISAIAH WROTE ABOUT THE REJECTION OF THE MESSIAH

"He is despised and rejected of men; a man of sorrows, and acquainted with grief: and we hid as it were our faces from him; he was despised, and we esteemed him not." **Isa.53:3 = John 1:11.**

ISAIAH WROTE THE MESSIAH BEING OUR SUBSTITUTE

"All we like sheep have gone astray; we have turned every one to his own way; and the Lord hath laid on him the iniquity of us all." **Isa.53:6 = 2 Cor.5:21.**

ISAIAH WROTE ABOUT THE MESSIAH'S WILLINGNESS TO SUFFER FOR HIS PEOPLE

"He was oppressed, and he was afflicted, yet he opened not his mouth: he is brought as a lamb to the slaughter, and as a sheep before her shearers is dumb, so he openeth not his mouth." **Isa.53:7 = John 1:29.**

ISAIAH WROTE ABOUT THE MESSIAH BEING BURIED WITH THE RICH

"And he made his grave with the wicked, and with the rich in his death." **Isa.53:9 = Matt.27:57-60.**

ISAIAH WROTE ABOUT THE MESSIAH SUFFERING WITH THE TRANSGRESSORS

"and he was numbered with the transgressors and he bare the sin of many, and made intercession for the transgressors." **Isa.53:12 = Luke 22:37, Luke 23:43, John 3:16.**

ISAIAH WROTE ABOUT THE MESSIAH HEALING THE BROKENHEARTED

"The Spirit of the Lord is upon me; because the Lord hath anointed me to preach good tidings unto the meek; he hath sent me to bind up the brokenhearted, to proclaim liberty to the captives, and the opening

of the prison to them that are bound; To proclaim the acceptable year of the Lord." **Isa.61:1-2a = Luke 4:18-19.**

Also, we know that **Isaiah 53** was referring to *Yeshua* the Messiah, because it was this passage that was explained to the Ethiopian eunuch in **Acts 8**, by the evangelist Philip.

MESSIAH IN JEREMIAH
(626-587BC ?)

The Hebrew name for *"Jeremiah,"* is *"Yirmeyahu,"* which means, *"Yah exalts."* He prophesied during the reign of the godly king Josiah, and helped him to reform much of the land of Israel. After his death, king Jehoahaz took the throne in Jerusalem, and was taken away into Egypt during the third month of his reign. Jeremiah saw the fall of Jerusalem and Solomon's temple destroyed. He preached to the poor that were left back in Jerusalem, and then followed the captives into Egypt where he died. He is believed to have written the books of Jeremiah, I and II Kings, and Lamentations. Jeremiah is also called the *"weeping prophet,"* because of the difficult message that he was called to deliver about the sins of his own people, and the persecution that he endured. He is considered the second major Prophet in the canon of the Hebrew scripture. Even though there are not as many passages in the book of Jeremiah that connect to the Messiah as Isaiah, the ones that we do find are very significant.

MESSIAH'S ATTACK FROM SATAN AT HIS BIRTH, WOULD BE A PARALLEL TO THE WEEPING OF RACHEL

"This saith the Lord; A voice was heard in Ramah, lamentation, and bitter weeping; Rahel weeping for her children refused to be comforted

for her children, because they were not." **Jere.31:15 = Matt.2:18.** **(Rachel was considered the mother of all of Israel, and the verse is saying that Rachel wept when her children (Israel) were taken into Babylonian captivity, also had a double meaning and was quoted during the time that Herod the Great killed the male children))**

MESSIAH WOULD BE A DESCENDANT OF DAVID

"Behold, the days come, saith the Lord, that I will raise unto David a righteous Branch, and a King shall reign and prosper, and shall execute judgment and justice in the earth." **Jere.23:5, 33:14-15, = Matt.1:1, Romans 1:3.**

MESSIAH WOULD BE YEHOVAH THE RIGHTEOUS ONE

"In his days Judah shall be saved, and Israel shall dwell safely: and this is his name whereby he shall be called, THE LORD OUR RIGHTEOUSNESS." **Jere.23:6 = Matt.5:6, Matt.6:20, 2 Cor.5:21.**

MESSIAH WOULD BE VIRGIN BORN

""How long wilt thou go about, O thou backsliding daughter? for the Lord hath created a new thing in the earth. A woman shall compass a man." **Jere.31:22 = Luke 1:34-35.**

MESSIAH WOULD BRING IN THE NEW COVENANT

"Behold, the days come, saith the Lord, that I will make a new covenant with the house of Israel, and with the house of Judah: Not

according to the covenant that I made with their fathers in the day that I took them by the hand to bring them out of the land of Egypt; which my covenant they brake, although I was an husband unto them, saith the Lord. But this shall be the covenant that I will make with the house of Israel; After those days, saith the Lord, I will put my law in their inward parts, and write it in their hearts; and will be their God, and they shall be my people. And they shall teach no more every man his neighbor, and every man his brother, saying, Know the Lord: for they shall all know me, from the least of them unto the greatest of them, saith the Lord: for I will forgive their iniquity, and I will remember their sin no more." **Jerte.31:31-34 = Matt.26:28, Hebrews 8:8-12.**

MESSIAH IN EZEKIEL
(598 – 570BC ?)

"Ezekiel," or the Hebrew *"Yechezk"el,"* which means, *"May God strengthen him."* The third one of the major Prophets, was fifty years old before he saw his first vision. Ezekiel is one of the few Prophets that prophesied outside of the land of Israel. After the destruction of the temple in Jerusalem, in 587BC, *(also recorded in Babylonian cuneiforms found by archaeologists)* he was taken away to Babylon between the first and final deportations of Judah. The book is filled with symbolism and visions, similar to the book of Daniel and the Revelation. Through Ezekiel, the God of Israel is speaking to the whole house of Israel. Over a period of twenty-two years, Ezekiel reminded the people of the sins that brought them into captivity, but also to the future kingdom and the national glory of David. Ezekiel heard the very *"voice of the Lord,"* and he saw Him with *"loins,"* with *"eyes,"* with *"ears,"* with *"hands,"* with *"feet,"* as the *"Son of man."* Woven throughout this seemingly comprehensive, visionary book, are countless pictures and symbols of the Messiah, let's look at some of the most intriguing.

EZEKIEL SAW THE LORD ON THE THRONE

"And above the firmament that was over their heads was the likeness of a throne, as the appearance of a sapphire stone: and upon the likeness of the throne was the likeness as the appearance of a man

51

above upon it. And I saw as the colour of amber, as the appearance of fire round about within it, from the appearance of his loins even upward, and from the appearance of his loins even downward, I saw as it were the appearance of fire, and it had brightness round about. As the appearance of the bow that is in the cloud in the day of rain, so was the appearance of the brightness round about. This was the appearance of the likeness of the glory of the Lord. And when I saw it, I fell upon my face, and I heard a voice of one that spoke." **Ezekiel 1:26-28 = Rev.1:12-18, Rev.4:3.**

EZEKIEL SAW THE MESSIAH AS A KING

"And I will make them one nation in the land upon the mountains of Israel; and one king shall be king to them all: and they shall be no more two nations, neither shall they be divided into two kingdoms any more at all." **Eze.37:22 = Luke 1:32.**

EZEKIEL SAW THE MESSIAH
THE SON OF DAVID

"And David my servant shall be over them." **Eze.37:24 = Matt.1:1.**

EZEKIEL SAW THE MESSIAH
AS BEING A SHEPHERD

"and they shall have one shepherd." **Eze.37:24 = John 10:11, I Peter 5:4.**

EZEKIEL SAW GOD'S GLORY
DEPARTING FROM JERUSALEM

"And the glory of the Lord went up from the midst of the city, and stood upon the mountain which is on the east side of the city." **Eze.11:23 = Matt.23:38-Matt.24:3.**

EZEKIEL SAW THE GLORY OF GOD COMING BACK TO JERUSALEM FROM THE EAST

"Afterward he brought me to the gate, even the gate that looketh toward the east: And, behold, the glory of the God of Israel came from the way of the east." **Eze.43:1-2 = Matt.21:1-11, Zechariah 14:4.**

EZEKIEL SAW THE MESSIAH AS THE HOLY ONE OF ISRAEL

"So I will make my holy name known in the midst of my people Israel; and I will not let them pollute my holy name any more: and the heathen shall know that I am the Lord, the Holy One in Israel." **Eze.39:7 = Luke 1:49, Luke 4:34, Rev.4:8.**

MESSIAH IN DANIEL
(607-534BC?)

The book of Daniel is considered to be an apocalyptic book, and is closely connected to the study of eschatology. His book is introductory to the New Testament prophecies, where we find themes such as, the man of sin revealed, the great tribulation, the return of the Messiah, and the final resurrection and the judgments. Daniel was led away captive into Babylon along with Judah, around 604BC, and his visions and experiences fall under the kings of Nebuchadnezzar, Belshazzar, Darius, and Cyrus. His visions sweep across the entire course of Gentile world-rule, to the end of history, and the establishment of the Messianic kingdom. There are only a few people in the Bible where we do not find anything negative about their character; Joseph, Samuel, and Daniel. Daniel proved his faithfulness during times of persecution, and he is the only one to whom God revealed the exact coming of the Messiah. Here are a few of the verses that point us to the Messiah.

FOURTH MAN IN THE FIRE

"He answered and said, Lo, I see four men loose, walking in the midst of the fire, and they have no hurt; and the form of the fourth is like the Son of God." **(This was a pre-incarnate *theophany* of the Messiah)**

THE WRITING ON THE WALL

"In the same hour came forth fingers of a man's hand, and wrote over against the candlestick upon the plaister of the wall of the king's palace: and the king saw the part of the hand that wrote." **(Regarding judgment, the picture of a hand writing can be connected to those who reject the Lord, Jeremiah 17:13, and to *Yeshua* the Messiah, writing on the ground, in John 8:6)**

SECOND COMING OF THE SON OF MAN

"I saw in the night visions, and, behold, one like the Son of man came with clouds of heaven, and came to the Ancient of Days, and they brought him near before him." **Daniel 7:13 = Matt.24:30, Rev.1:12-18.**

EXACT TIME OF THE MESSIAH'S COMING

"Know therefore and understand, that from the going forth of the commandment to restore and to build Jerusalem unto the Messiah the Prince shall be seven weeks, and threescore and two weeks: the street shall be built again, and the wall, even in troublous times. And after threescore and two weeks shall Messiah be cut off, but not for himself." **Daniel 10:25-26.**

This is one of the most profound passages in the Old Testament, and even though it sounds very hard to understand, I will try to simplify it for you, so you can see how important it is. The Messiah will come 483 years after the decree is signed to rebuild Jerusalem. When we read **Nehemiah 2:1-8**, we find that this decree was signed by Artaxerxes, the king of the Medo-Persian Empire during the first month, Nissan, or what we know as the month of April; in the twentieth year of his reign, which was the year 445BC.

So when we add 483 years to 445BC, using 360-day years, *(this is how long the years were when God created everything in Genesis)* we come to the first week of April, in 32AD, when the Messiah was crucified, **(cut off).** When we carefully study the timeline of *Yeshua's* public ministry, we see that He was thirty years old when He was baptized, **Luke 3:23,** and this was during the fifteenth year of the reign of Tiberius Caesar, **Luke 3:1-2,** which was the second half of the year **28AD**. *(Tiberius Caesar started to reign in August of 14AD, after the death of Augustus Caesar)* So if we figure the date of *Yeshua's* birth at 2BC, *(also by studying Egyptian and Roman history along with the Bible)* then *Yeshua* would have been 33 ½ years of age at the time of His death in Jerusalem. We shouldn't be surprised with the accuracy of Daniel's prophecy, for God's word is always true, even when we do not understand it with our finite minds.

MESSIAH IN THE
MINOR PROPHETS

The Minor Prophets are Hosea, Joel, Amos, Obadiah, Jonah, Micah, Nahum, Habakkuk, Zephaniah, Haggai, Zechariah, and Malachi. With the Major and Minor Prophets combined, it has been said that there are 243 verses in the Prophets that speak of the Messiah directly. When reading the Prophets we need to be reminded that the Prophets searched diligently to understand the meanings of the scriptures they were inspired to write.

"Of which salvation the prophets have inquired and searched diligently, who prophesied of the grace that should come unto you. Searching what, or what manner of time the Spirit of Christ which was in them did signify, when it testified beforehand the sufferings of Christ, and the glory that should follow." **I Peter 1:10-11.**

While preaching on the Day of Pentecost, Simon Peter told the people that it was clearly written in the Prophets about the first coming of the Messiah.

"Yea, and all the prophets from Samuel and those that follow after, as many as have spoken, have likewise foretold of these days." **Acts 3:24.**

However, the Prophets struggled with the *sufferings* and the *glory* of the coming Messiah of Israel. *Sufferings*; referring to all that the Messiah suffered during His first coming, mainly the cross, and the *glories*; which could be referring to His resurrection, or His ascension, or His glorification, or His return, or the Davidic Kingdom that He would establish. The Holy Spirit was in them, giving them what to write, but they had limited revelation. God was using them even though they did not fully understand these mysterious truths.

These so-called contradictions have caused many of the Jewish rabbis to teach a two-Messiah view in rabbinic literature. Because they too were unable to reconcile the two themes of *suffering* and *glory*, they created the "Messiah, the son of Joseph," who would fulfill the suffering Messiah, and the "Messiah, the son of David," who would fulfill the ruling and reigning Messiah. But of course the New Testament makes it clear that there is only one Messiah, *Yeshua*!

Many of the minor Prophets of Israel used terms such as, *"Behold, the days come,"* or *"at the end of the days,"* or *"in the last days,"* as they were writing about the second coming of the Messiah. We find these reoccurring themes throughout their prophetic writings. Also, we find that sometimes a Prophet was preaching to backsliding Israel, and woven within the text, is a picture of a greater fulfillment that would happen in the life of the Messiah. These complicated, but true, deeper interpretations, have caused many of the religious Jews, to this very day, to ignore and even refuse to read some of the Prophets. Once again, I will try to give you a brief summary of some of the Messianic prophecies and fulfillments; this time searching through the Minor Prophets.

HOSEA = *"Hoshea"* (8th Century BC)

"I will go and return to my place, till they acknowledge their offence, and seek my face: in their affliction they will seek me early." **Hosea 5:15 = Matt.23:39.**

"When Israel was a child, then I loved him, and called my son out of Egypt." **Hosea 11:1 = Matt.2:15.**

JOEL = *"Yo'el"* (9th Century BC)

"And I will shew wonders in the heavens and in the earth, blood, and fire, and pillars of smoke. The sun shall be turned into darkness, and the moon into blood, before the great and terrible day of the Lord come." **Joel 2:30-31 = Matt.24:29-30.**

"And it shall come to pass, that whosoever shall call on the name of the Lord shall be delivered." **Joel 2:32 = Acts 2:20-21, Romans 10:13.**

AMOS = *" 'Amos"* (8th Century BC)

"And it shall come to pass in that day, saith the Lord God, that I will cause the sun to go down at noon, and I will darken the earth in the clear day." **Amos 8:9 = Matt.27:45.**

"In that day will I raise up the tabernacle of David that is fallen, and closed up the breaches thereof; and I will raise up his ruins, and I will build it was in the days of old: That they may possess the remnant of Edom, and of all the heathen, which are called by my name, saith the Lord that doeth this. Behold, the days come, saith the Lord, that the plowman shall overtake the reaper, and the treader of grapes him that soweth seed; and the mountains shall drop sweet wine, and all the hills shall melt. And I will bring again the captivity of my people of Israel, and they shall build the waste cities, and inhabit them; and they shall plant vineyards, and drink the wine thereof; they shall also

make gardens, and eat the fruit of them. And I will plant them upon their land, and they shall no more be pulled up out of their land which I have given them, saith the Lord thy God." **Amos 9:11-15 = Acts 1:6, Acts 15:16-17."**

OBADIAH = *"Ovadhah"* (9ᵗʰ Century BC)

"For the day of the Lord is near upon all the heathen: as thou hast done, it shall be done unto thee: thy reward shall return upon thine own head." **Obadiah 15 = Rev.16:14-16.**

JONAH = *"Yonah"* (9ᵗʰ Century BC)

"Now the Lord had prepared a great fish to swallow up Jonah. And Jonah was in the belly of the fish three days and three nights." **Jonah 1:17 = Matt.12:39-40.**

MICAH = *"Mikhah"* (8ᵗʰ Century BC)

"But thou, Beth-lehem Ephratah, though thou be little among the thousands of Judah, yet out of thee shall he come forth unto me that is to be ruler in Israel; whose goings forth have been from of old, from everlasting." **Micah 5:2 = Matt.2:6.**

NAHUM = *"Nachum"* (8ᵗʰ Century BC)

"The Lord is slow to anger, and great in power, and will not at all acquit the wicked." **Nahum 1:3 = Romans 3:26.**

HABAKKUK = *"Havakuk"* (7ᵗʰ Century BC)

"His glory covered the heavens, and the earth was full of his praise. And his brightness was as the light; he had horns (rays) coming out of

his hand: and there was the hiding of his power." **Habakkuk 3:3-4 = Matt.24:30, Rev.5:1-7.**

ZEPHANIAH = *"Tz' fanyah"* (7th Century BC)

"for the day of the Lord is at hand: for the Lord hath prepared a sacrifice, he hath bid his guests." **Zephaniah 1:7**

"The great day of the Lord is near, it is near, and hasteth greatly, even the voice of the day of the Lord: the mighty man shall cry there bitterly." **Zephaniah 1:14 = Rev.19:11-21.**

HAGGAI = *"Hagai"* (6TH Century BC)

"The glory of this latter house shall be greater than the former, saith the Lord of hosts: and in this place will I give peace, saith the Lord of hosts." **Haggai 2:9 = Luke 2:21-32.**

"In that day, saith the Lord of hosts, will I take thee, O Zerubbabel, my servant, the son of Shealtiel, saith the Lord, and will make thee as a signet: for I have chosen thee, saith the Lord of hosts." **Haggai 2:23 = Luke 3:27.**

ZECHARIAH = *"Z'kharyah"* (6th Century BC)

"Rejoice greatly, O daughter of Zion; shout, O daughter of Jerusalem: behold, thy King cometh unto thee: her is just, and having salvation; lowly, and riding upon an ass, and upon the colt the foal of an ass." **Zechariah 9:9 = John 12:14-15.**

"So they weighed for my price thirty pieces of silver. And the Lord said unto me, Cast it unto the potter: a goodly price that I was prised at of them. And I took thirty pieces of silver, and cast them to the potter

in the house of the Lord." **Zechariah 11:12-13 = Matt.26:15, Matt.27:10.**

"And I will pour upon the house of David, and upon the inhabitants of Jerusalem, the spirit of grace and of supplications: and they shall look upon me whom they have pierced, and they shall mourn for him, as one mourneth for his only son, and shall be in bitterness for him, as one that is in bitterness for his firstborn." **Zechariah 12:10 = John 19:37, Rev.1:7.**

"And his feet shall stand in that day upon the mount of Olives, which is before Jerusalem on the east, and the mount of Olives shall cleave in the midst thereof toward the east and toward the west, and there shall be a very great valley; and half of the mountain shall remove toward the north, and half of it toward the south." **Zechariah 14:4 = Acts 1:10-12.**

MALACHI = *"Mal'akhi"* (4th Century BC)

"Behold, l will send my messenger, and he shall prepare the way before me: and the Lord, whom ye seek, shall suddenly come to his temple, even the messenger of the covenant, whom ye delight in: behold, he shall come, saith the Lord of hosts." **Malachi 3:1 = Mark 1:2.**

"Behold, I will send you Elijah the prophet before the coming of the great and dreadful day of the Lord: And he shall turn the heart of the fathers to the children, and the heart of the children to their fathers, lest I come and smite the earth with a curse." **Malachi 4:5-6 = Matt.17:10-13.**

MESSIAH IN THE BOOK OF ENOCH (300-200BC?)

MESSIAH RETURNS IN JUDGMENT

"And, behold! He cometh with ten thousand of holy ones to execute judgement upon all, And to destroy all the ungodly." **I Enoch 1:9**

"And Enoch also, the seventh from Adam, prophesied of these, saying, Behold, the Lord cometh with ten thousand of his saints, To execute judgment upon all, and to convince all that are ungodly among them of all their ungodly deeds which they have ungodly committed, and of all their hard speeches which ungodly sinners have spoken against him." **Jude 14-15.**

The book of Enoch was written during the intertestamental period, between the book of Malachi and the New Testament. While no Prophet thundered in the land of Israel during this four hundred year period, I do find this particular book to hold some value. I do not see how any open-minded Bible scholar can discount completely the apocryphal book of Enoch. True, it is not in the canon of scripture, but when one of the New Testament authors quotes from this book we need to re-visit the inspiration of Enoch. Jude is not saying that the entire book of Enoch is inspired by God, but he is giving his approval on at least *some* of the book. Enoch, was the seventh from Adam, and during the three hundred and sixty five years that he lived, he walked so close to God, that God took him, and Enoch did not see death, **Gen.5:23-24**. I have no reason to doubt that someone who was so close to God, could have written this book and that it has been preserved for a reason. There are ten fragments of this book that were found in the Dead Sea Scrolls that were discovered in 1947. The book was written in Hebrew and Aramaic.

MESSIAH IN THE
GOSPELS (2BC- 32AD)

As we come to the four gospels, it is important to understand that the religious establishment that was in place during the life of *Yeshua* the Messiah would be judged by the very same scriptures that they claimed to live by. Like many of the unbelieving, religious Jews of our day, they focused more on a national Israel, their interpretations of the Torah, and rabbinical thought, more than they did a *personal* Messiah. However, we have seen from the *Torah,* the *Prophets,* the *Psalms,* and some historical writings, as well as the approximately four hundred year intertestamental period, that a personal Messiah was prophesied. It is clear that an individual Messiah of Israel had to be a Jew, **Matt.1:1,** through the lineage of king David, **Matt.22:41-46,** and that He would also be the God of Abraham, Isaac, and Jacob, in human form, **Isa.9:6, John 8:58.** It is also clear that the Messiah of Israel had to come through the village of *Bethlehem-Ephrathah,* **Micah 5:2,** in the south, and that He would grow up as a *Nazarene,* **Isa.11:1,** in the north, and have His ministry headquarters in the *Galilee,* **Isa.9:1-2,** before suffering for the sins of the world in Jerusalem, **Psalm 22, Isa.53, Luke 13:33.**

In the midst of the corrupt, religious establishment of the Sadducees and the Pharisees, there was a remnant that was living in expectation of the coming Messiah. We can see this when Mary and Joseph brought the baby *Yeshua* to the temple in Jerusalem.

"And, behold, there was a man in Jerusalem, whose name was Simeon; and the same man was just and devout, <u>waiting for the consolation of Israel</u>: and the Holy Ghost was upon him." **Luke 2:25.**

"And she coming in that instant gave thanks likewise unto the Lord, and <u>spake of him to all them that looked for redemption in Jerusalem</u>." **Luke 2:38.**

We find the word *"Christ,"* over sixty times in the four gospels. As we mentioned before, this word comes from the Greek, *"christos,"* which means *"anointed."* When the Hebrew *"Mashiach,"* was transliterated into the Greek, the result was "Messias," **John 1:41, John 4:25.** The word *"Messiah,"* is an anglicized form of the Greek transliteration of the Hebrew word *"Mashiach,"* **Daniel 9:25-26.**

It is also important to point out that modern Christianity has attempted to remove the political and nationalistic parts of the Messiah, and only focus on the ethical and spiritual parts. We see many times the connection of *Yeshua* riding the donkey with **Zech.9:9**, but we fail to see the political expectation during the triumphal entry, in **Matt.21:9.** The people were hoping for a Messiah who would set them free from Roman oppression.

"And the multitudes that went before, and that followed, cried, saying, Hosanna **(the Hebrew *Hoshana* means, "save, rescue, savior")** *to the son of David: Blessed is he that cometh in the name of the Lord; Hosanna in the highest."*

Yeshua was met with the expectation of a military, conquering Messiah during His public ministry. He was certainly aware of the

Roman occupation that fueled the fires of Messianic fever among His own people. *Yeshua* knew about the wide variety of ideas and notions concerning the coming Messiah, but His message transcended all of those ideas. One needs to take in consideration the many different Messianic beliefs among the common people, as well as the religious groups of the day, and how that had an impact on how *Yeshua* chose to teach and present Himself. This helps us to understand better why there were times that *Yeshua* chose to not identify who He was, **Mark 1:44, Mark 5:43.** *Yeshua* was confident in Himself of who He was, but He knew that He had only a small window of opportunity to finish the work that He was sent to do. His cautiousness was to avoid some of the misunderstandings of His day concerning the role of the Messiah, as well as, He wanted to provoke mental effort on the part of His listeners.

The titles, such as *"Son of Man,"* and *"Son of God,"* were just as Messianic as a direct claim that He was the Messiah. The title, *"Son of God,"* connected *Yeshua* to passages like **Isa.9:6** and **Proverbs 30:4.** The title, *"Son of Man,"* connected *Yeshua* back to verses like **Daniel 7:13-14.**

When we look at all of the *"I Am,"* statements of *Yeshua*, He was identifying Himself with the God of the Old Testament. The title, *"the light of the world,"* in **John 8:12,** clearly connected *Yeshua* to the God of Israel from places like **Psalm 27:1** and **Isa.42:6.** The title, *"I am the bread of life,"* in **John 6:48,** was explained by *Yeshua* to be the primary meaning of the feeding of the 5,000, plus the fulfillment of the *manna* in the wilderness, **Exo.16:35.** The title, *"I am the good shepherd,"* in **John 10:11,** connected *Yeshua* to the God of Israel who shepherds His people, **Psalm 23.** One of the most provocative titles that *Yeshua* ever used was in **John 8:58,** and after He made that claim, they took of stones to cast at him, because *Yeshua* was clearly identifying Himself with the God of Abraham.

"Jesus said unto them, Verily, verily, I say unto you, Before Abraham was, I am."

There are other factors that support *Yeshua's* claim to be the Messiah. When *Yeshua* taught from the law of Moses, He taught like no other rabbi, by comparing their Oral law to, *"But I say unto you,"* *Yeshua* was setting Himself as the supreme authority in interpreting the Holy scripture.

When *Yeshua* told the palsied man *"Thy sins are forgiven,"* in **Mark 2:9,** He was clearly identifying Himself as the God of Israel who forgives sin, **Psalm 32:1-2.**

When *Yeshua* cleansed the temple in Jerusalem in **John 2:16,** He said, *"Take these things hence; make not my Father's house an house of merchandise,"* the disciples later remembered, through the help of the Holy Spirit, *"The zeal of thine house hath eaten me up,"* from **Psalm 69:9.**

In **John 2:19,** while *Yeshua* was on the temple mount in Jerusalem, He said, *"Destroy this temple, and in three days I will raise it up,"* and this statement made such an impact on the religious rulers that they brought it up as an accusation three years later when *Yeshua* was on the cross, in **Matt.27:40.**

Andrew, the brother of Simon Peter, certainly saw in Yeshua the Messianic hopes he had been longing for. When he came to tell his brother Simon about *Yeshua*, notice the first thing that he said:

"He first findeth his own brother Simon, and saith unto him, We have found the Messias, which is, being interpreted, the Christ." **John 1:41.**

The disciple Philip describes *Yeshua* to Nathanael as the one who was prophesied about in the Hebrew scriptures.

"Philip findeth Nathanael, and saith unto him, We have found him, of whom Moses in the law, and the prophets, did write, Jesus of Nazareth, the son of Joseph." **John 1:45.**

After Nathanael realized that *Yeshua* had the supernatural knowledge of seeing him under the fig tree even before they met, he proclaimed:

"Nathanael answered and saith unto him, Rabbi, thou art the Son of God; thou art the King of Israel." **John 1:49.**

Yeshua told the religious ruler Nicodemus that He was the fulfillment of the brazen serpent on the pole, in **John 3:14, Numbers 21:9.** *Yeshua* also called Himself in this verse, *"the Son of man."*

One of the most profound chapters in the gospels is when *Yeshua* was talking to the Samaritan woman, and *Yeshua* knew that she was expecting a personal Messiah who would have all wisdom and knowledge. Listen to the expectation in the woman's heart and then listen to *Yeshua's* reply.

"The woman saith unto him, I know that Messias cometh, which is called Christ: when he is come, he will tell us all things. Jesus saith unto her, I that speak unto thee am he." **John 4:25-26.**

After the woman went into the village, many others believed after they heard *Yeshua* for themselves.

"Now we believe, not because of thy saying: for we have heard him ourselves, and know that this is indeed the Christ, the Saviour of the world." **John 4:42.**

After *Yeshua* gave the sermon about *"eating his flesh, and drinking his blood,"* **John 6:53-56,** in the synagogue at Capernaum, many of His disciples turned back and walked no more with Him. Simon Peter spoke for the other disciples and said the reason why they would not turn back because they knew that He was the Messiah.

"Then said Jesus unto the twelve, will ye also go away? Then Simon Peter answered him, Lord, to whom shall we go? thou hast the words of eternal life. And we believe and are sure that thou art the Christ, the Son of the living God." **John 6:67-69.**

There was a division among the people in Jerusalem when some said that *Yeshua* was the Prophet that Moses wrote about, while others said that He was the Messiah. Some argued that the Messiah should come from Bethlehem, and not Galilee. If they had of known the sacred scriptures better they would have known the prophecies concerning the Galilean ministry of the Messiah, in **Isa.9:1-2.**

"Many of the people therefore, when they heard this saying, said, Of a truth this is the Prophet. Others said, This is the Christ. But some said, Shall Christ come out of Galilee? Hath not the scripture said, That Christ cometh of the seed of David, and out of the town of Bethlehem, where David was?" **John 7:40-42.**

Another amazing Messianic claim was seen in the events of the last Passover. When *Yeshua* broke the *matzoh*, and gave it to His disciples, and when He took the cup and gave it to the disciples, He was declaring that He was Passover Lamb, who had come to take away the sins of the world. **Exo.12, John 1:29.** In the same setting, *Yeshua* also reminded His disciples that He would return and establish the Messianic kingdom.

"And as they were eating, Jesus took bread, and blessed it, and brake it, and gave it to the disciples, and said, Take, eat; this is my body. And he took the cup, and gave thanks, and gave it to them, saying, Drink ye all of it; For this is my blood of the new testament, which is shed for many for the remission of sins. But I say unto you, I will not drink henceforth of this fruit of the vine, until that day when I drink it new with you in my Father's kingdom." **Matt.26:26-29.**

In one sense, all of the miracles that *Yeshua* performed were Messianic. Years ago, the Hebrew scholar, Arnold Fruchtenbaum, wrote about the miracles that were truly Messianic in nature. He mentions only three particular miracles, but I would like to give you his list, plus a few other miracles that I think should be included, that most definitely proved that *Yeshua* was the Messiah.

CLEANSING A LEPER

"And it came to pass, when he was in a certain city, behold a man full of leprosy: who seeing Jesus fell on his face, and besought him, saying, Lord, if thou wilt, thou canst make me clean. And he put forth his hand, and touched him, saying, I will: be thou clean. And immediately the leprosy departed from him." **Luke 5:12-13.**

Notice that this poor man was *"full of leprosy,"* and notice that the leper put forth the question to *Yeshua, "if thou wilt."* Touching a leper would make someone unclean under the Law of Moses, **Lev.13-14.** The question has to be asked; why put at least two chapters in the Bible about what a leper is supposed to do when he is cleansed, when it was so rare, or never happened in the history of Israel? The answer lies within the ministry of the coming Messiah, for only He could cleanse an unclean leper, thus proving His Messiahship.

There are several cases in the gospels where *Yeshua* touched someone who was unclean without defiling Himself. The encounter that *Yeshua* had with the maniac of Gadara, in **Mark 5:1-20,** revealed that *Yeshua* was in unclean, Gentile territory, with an unclean man who was filled with demons, who was living among the unclean tombs. There was the unclean woman with the issue of blood in **Mark 5:25-34,** as well as, the unclean daughter of *Jairus,* who had died in **Mark 5:41.**

Since the Law of Moses had been written, there had never been a Jewish leper who had been cleansed in the history of Israel. We have the case of *Miriam* who was healed of leprosy in **Num.12,** but this was a result of her speaking against Moses for marrying an Ethiopian woman, and God punished *Miriam* with leprosy, and she remained outside of the camp for seven days. The cleansing of *Naaman,* in **2 Kings 5,** is also mentioned by *Yeshua* in **Luke 4:27.** But we must remember that he was a Syrian and not Jewish. The rabbis in Bible times had no cure for leprosy. It was their thinking that only Israel's Messiah could cleanse a leper; and they were right. This healing of the leper was so important to the Messianic expectations of the day, that *Yeshua* sent him back to the priests to do whatever Moses commanded in the law, **Mark 1:44.** Evidently, the priests did not believe that *Yeshua* was the Messiah, and that showed how spiritually blinded they were. Immediately after the cleansing of the leper, in **Luke 5:17**, there were religious leaders gathered from every town in Galilee and Judaea, and *"the power of the Lord was present to heal them."* Just like *Yeshua* was willing to cleanse the Jewish leper, He was also willing to cleanse the religious rulers if they had of believed in Him. It was the custom that they would listen to the teaching and see the works of any messianic movement that started in the region. If the movement was truly Messianic in their minds, then they would come back to Jerusalem and bring it before the Sanhedrin. So, evidently, they thought that *Yeshua's* cleansing of the leper was Messianic in nature. From this day forward the religious rulers would follow *Yeshua* and try to find something of which they could accuse Him.

EXORCISM OF A MUTE, DEMON POSSESSED MAN

"Then was brought unto him one possessed with a devil, blind, and dumb: and he healed him, insomuch that the blind and dumb both spake and saw: And all the people were amazed, and said, Is not this the Son of David?" **Matt.12:22-23.**

Casting out demons was performed by many of the rabbis in *Yeshua's* time, **Matt.12:27,** but no one could cast the demon out of anyone who could not speak. The rabbis said that when the true Messiah comes, then that kind of demon would be cast out, but not until. In most cases, the exorcist would ask the name of the demon, and the demon would speak, like in **Mark 5:9**. Then, by speaking the name of the demon, the demon would be cast out. But in this case, the demon could not speak, and there was no way of establishing any communication between the one doing the exorcism and the demon. This miracle proved the King Messiah had arrived and the kingdom of God had come. Notice the words of the prophet Isaiah, concerning the kingdom age:

"and the tongue of the dumb sing." **Isa.35:6.**

It is very interesting that after this Messianic miracle, the people were amazed, and asked, *"Is not this the son of David?"* The people knew that this was a miracle that only the Messiah could perform. Why did they not receive *Yeshua* as their long awaited Messiah? Because of the strong influence of rabbinical Judaism, that was handed down through the scribes and Pharisees. The religious leaders denounced *Yeshua*, and said that He performed this miracle through the power of the devil. This miracle led to the national, unpardonable sin of Israel, accusing their Messiah of being filled with Satan. The *unpardonable sin* is not an individual sin, but a national sin. These verses are noteworthy, because it was a major transition in the ministry of the Messiah, and would eventually lead to His crucifixion in Jerusalem. This also set the stage for the next two thousand years, and most religious Jews today still believe that *Yeshua* was demon possessed.

"But when the Pharisees heard it, they said, This fellow doth not cast out devils, but by Beelzebub the prince of devils. And Jesus knew their thoughts, and said unto them, Every kingdom divided against itself is brought to desolation; and every city or house divided against itself shall not stand. And if Satan cast out Satan, he is divided against himself; how shall then his kingdom stand? And if I by Beelzebub cast out devils, by whom do your children cast them out? therefore they shall be your judges. But if I cast out devils by the Spirit of God, then the kingdom of God is come unto you. Or else how can one enter into a strong man's house, and spoil his goods, except he first bind the strong man? and then he will spoil his house." **Matt.12:24-29.**

This rejection by the religious leaders brought about a change in the ministry of the Messiah in four ways:

1) *His miracles would shift from proving His Messiahship to training and equipping His disciples.*
2) *Before this miracle, sometimes Yeshua would not ask for a demonstration of faith, but after, He only performed miracles on the basis of individual faith.*
3) *After this miracle, Yeshua would tell the people, "Don't tell anyone," more emphatically.*
4) *From this moment on, Yeshua began to conceal His teaching by way of parables.*

THE HEALING OF A MAN BORN BLIND

"And as Jesus passed by, he saw a man which was blind from his birth. And his disciples asked him, saying, Master, who did sin, this man, or his parents, that he was born blind?" Jesus answered, Neither hath this man sinned, nor his parents: but that the works of God should be made manifest in him. I must work the works of him that sent me, while it is day: the night cometh, when no man can work. As long as I am in the world, I am the light of the world. When he had thus spoken, he spat on the ground, and made clay of the spittle, and he anointed the eyes of the blind man with the clay. And said unto him, Go, wash in the pool of Siloam, (which is by interpretation, Sent.) He went his way therefore, and washed, and came seeing." **John 9:1-7.**

"Since the world began was it not heard that any man opened the eyes of one that was born blind." **John 9:32.**

It was a common thought among the rabbis, that only the Messiah could heal anyone that was *born* blind. It was also the common thought of the day among the rabbis, that someone who was *born* blind, or who was born with a birth defect, must be the result of sin in the life of the person or sin in the life of the family. This came from their their interpretation of **Exo.34:6-7**. But *Yeshua* dismantled this logic! Sin is a result of the fall of man, and physical imparities are not *always* connected to a certain sin. God was going to receive glory and honor from this man who had been born blind.

The way that *Yeshua* chose to heal this man who was born blind is very interesting to me. He chose to make *spittle* out of clay, and then He sent this man to a certain pool, the *pool of Siloam*. In Jewish thought, the spittle of a firstborn, male child, had supernatural powers. Was *Yeshua* saying that He was the firstborn of the virgin Mary, and He was also the firstbotten Son of God? This miracle took place on the Jewish Sabbath day, during the Jewish Feast of Tabernacles. One of the highlights of this fall feast was for a priest to take a golden pitcher down to the old city of David, and go to the pool of Siloam and fill it with water. He would bring the water back and pour it on the altar, as a way of praising the God of Israel for His provision of rain, and asking the God of Israel to provide water during the coming winter. All of the religious leaders in Jerusalem were gathered at the pool of Siloam for this once in a year celebration. This miracle was not only to bring glory to God but to also show the spiritual blindness of the religious leaders in Jerusalem. The Pharisees not only condemned *Yeshua* for performing this miracle on the Sabbath day, **John 9:16,** but they excommunicated this poor man, **(known as the Hebrew *"cherem"*)** out of the synagogue, **John 9:34**, which was the worst form of punishment in every day Jewish life. Not only did *Yeshua* heal this man physically, but after He found out that they had excommunicated the man, He healed him spiritually,

John 9:35-38. Three important results occurred from these first three Messianic miracles:

1) *Investigation* **(Healing of the leper)**
2) *Rejection* of their Messiah **(Healing of the mute, demon possessed man)**
3) *Excommunication* **(Healing of the man born blind, anyone who believed in Yeshua was cast out)**

Again, we need to connect the healing of the man born blind to miracles that are listed in **Isa.35**, because they are kingdom-related miracles.

"Then the eyes of the blind shall be opened." **Isa.35:5.**

RAISING OF LAZARUS AFTER FOUR DAYS

"Jesus said, Take ye away the stone. Martha, the sister of him that was dead, saith unto him, Lord, by this time he stinketh: for he hath been dead four days." **John 11:39.**

"And when he thus had spoken, he cried with a loud voice, Lazarus, come forth. And he that was dead came forth, bound hand and foot with graveclothes: and his face was bound about with a napkin. Jesus saith unto them, Loose him, and let him go." **John 11:43-44.**

Yeshua had raised *Jairus'* daughter from the dead, as well as, the widow's son in Nain, **Mark 5:41, Luke 7:11-18.** But in the raising of *Lazarus* from Bethany, after *Yeshua* heard about his death, He deliberately waited two extra days beyond Jordan, which was over twenty miles away, **John 11:6**. Coming from the Jordan River, *Yeshua* would have come into Bethany before entering into Jerusalem, because it was on the eastern slope of the Mt. of Olives.

It was the common thought among the rabbis, that after four days the spirit had departed the body and there was no way to revive a person who had been in the grave this long. Once the body had started to decompose, they believed the body was totally separated from the spirit. Within this pericope of **John 11**, we find two important verses:

"Martha saith unto him, I know that he shall rise again in the resurrection at the last day. Jesus said unto her, I am the resurrection, and the life: he that believeth in me, though he were dead, yet shall he live." **John 11:24-25.**

"Jesus wept." **John 11:35.**

Yeshua was going to prove that He not only had the power to raise a dead man who had been dead for four days, but that He was *the resurrection* Himself! He would show through this miracle, that everyone who embraces Him as the Messiah, will live eternally. Though we will die in the flesh, life with our Lord will continue. This miracle would also be a picture of that glorious, resurrection day when the Messiah returns and all of His people will be raised in glory, and their bodies will meet their spirit in the air, and when we will have a glorified body just like our Lord. Again, if we die before the Messiah returns, our spirit goes to be with the Lord, and one day our bodies will reunite with the spirit on that resurrection morning. Notice this verse in the book of Daniel:

"And many of them that sleep in the dust of the earth shall awake, some to everlasting life, and some to shame and everlasting contempt." **Dan.12:2.**

The fact that *Yeshua wept* has brought on many conjectures over the centuries. But it certainly showed His love for this family who lived in Bethany, where He had visited on other occasions, **Luke 10:38-42, John 12:1-8.** The tears of the Messiah showed the strange mystery of Him being both God and Man, and that He could feel the sorrow that every human feels in this life. It could also mean that *Yeshua's* heart was broken as He saw what sin had brought into the world. He desired for man to live forever, and sin interrupted His plan for mankind. **(Man lived to be over 900 years old, Gen. 5, even after the fall, before other diseases entered into the blood stream of man)** *Yeshua* the Messiah came to give His children the assurance that they would live forever with Him.

The raising of Lazarus had such an impact on the people, that many believed on Him as a result, **John 11:45, John 12:11**, and the corrupt, religious rulers became afraid that their positions of authority among the people was going to come crashing down, **John 11:48**. This led to a very important, and strange prophecy that was spoken through the high priest *Caiaphas*; that included not only the believing Jews but also the believing Gentiles in the future; even though he didn't really understand what he was saying.

"And one of them, named Caiaphas, being the high priest that same year, said unto them, Ye know nothing at all, Nor consider that it is expedient for us, that one man should die for the people, and that the whole nation perish not. And this spake he not of himself: but being high priest that year, he prophesied that Jesus should die for that nation; And not for that nation only, but that also he should gather together in one the children of God that were scattered abroad." **John 11:49-52.**

When we read on to **John 12,** we one of the most beautiful pictures. We find Mary, Martha, and Lazarus, together with their Lord.

"Then Jesus six days before the Passover came to Bethany, where Lazarus was which had been dead, whom he raised from the dead. There they made him a supper; and Martha served: but Lazarus was one of them that sat at the table with him. Then took Mary a pound of ointment of spikenard, very costly, and anointed the feet of Jesus, and wiped his feet with her hair: and the house was filled with the odour of the ointment." **John 12:1-3.**

After the raising of Lazarus, the religious leaders were consulting how they could put *Yeshua* to death, as well as Lazarus, because many believed in *Yeshua* as a result of the miracle. But we must never forget that while the enemy wages war, the true children of God are having sweet fellowship with their Lord. Notice the spiritual applications for us here:

1) *Lazarus* = Fellowship
2) *Martha* = Service
3) *Mary* = Worship

THE ULTIMATE MESSIANIC MIRACLE

"Then delivered he him therefore unto them to be crucified. And they took Jesus, and led him away." **John 19:16.**

"He is not here, but is risen." **Luke 24:6.**

Yet, there remains one final Messianic miracle; the death, the burial, and the resurrection of the Messiah. If it were not for this miracle, then everything else would be meaningless. Even though it was the least understood prophecy, it was clear in the writings of the Psalms and the Prophets that Israel's Messiah had to be a *suffering servant*. This was the sword that would pierce through the heart of the mother Mary that was spoken of by Simeon at the temple in Jerusalem.

("Yea, a sword shall pierce through thy own soul also,) that the thoughts of many hearts may be revealed." **Luke 2:35.**

All of the other miracles and all of the mysterious parables could not save a lost world. All of the blood sacrifices in the old economy would find their fulfillment in the death of the Messiah. But every time when *Yeshua* talked about His death, He always talked about His glorious resurrection. *Yeshua* had foretold His pending death and resurrection, starting in the region of Caesarea Philippi, after Simon Peter's great confession.

"From that time forth began Jesus to shew unto his disciples, how that he must go unto Jerusalem, and suffer many things of the elders and chief priests and scribes, and be killed, and be raised again the third day." **Matt.16:21.**

When *Yeshua* was transfigured on the Mt. of Transfiguration, His death and resurrection was the subject that Moses and Elijah were discussing with Him.

"And, behold, there talked with him two men, which were Moses and Elias: Who appeared in glory, and spake of his decease (exodus) which he should accomplish at Jerusalem." **Luke 9:30-31.**

The primary purpose of the incarnation was for the Messiah to be able to be man's representative in death. When the wise men brought gifts to Him at His birth; of gold, frankincense, and myrrh; they were symbols of what was to happen a little over thirty three years later, at His burial, **Matt.2:11, John 19:39**. In the Jordan River, when He was baptized, it was to be identified with His people, and to be identified with His own pending death. Throughout His earthly ministry, *Yeshua* was very much aware of His mission and He knew the time and place when it was all coming down.

"And it came to pass, when the time was come that he should be received up, he stedfastly set his face to go to Jerusalem." **Luke 9:51.**

All of the sins of the world had to be paid for, and the Holy justice of the universe had to be met. There was only *One* who could perform this miracle, *Yeshua* the Messiah! *Yeshua* had to take away the sins of the world, **John 1:29**. A perfect sacrifice from heaven's glory is the only way that He could provide righteousness for His people.

"And he is the propitiation for our sins: and not for ours only, but also for the sins of the whole world." **I John 2:2.**

"To declare, I say, at this time his righteousness: that he might be just, and the justifier of him that believeth in Jesus." **Rom.3:26.**

"Who his own self bare our sins in his own body on the tree." **I Peter 2:24.**

"that he by the grace of God should taste death for every man." **Heb.2:9.**

"For he hath made him to be sin for us, who knew no sin; that we might be made the righteousness of God in him." **2 Cor.5:21.**

The *seed of the woman* (*Yeshua* the Messiah) had to bruise the head of the serpent, **Gen.3:15**. The seed of Satan could not prevent the seed of the woman (*Yeshua* the Messiah) from coming into the world, and he could not prevent Him from going to the cross. The works of Satan had to be defeated.

"And having spoiled principalities and powers, he made a shew of them openly, triumphing over them in it." **Col.2:15.**

"For this purpose the Son of God was manifested, that he might destroy the works of the devil." **I John 3:8.**

Israel's Messiah would have to be lifted up from the earth in order to fulfill the prophecies. And this uplifted Messiah would be the way for His people to be redeemed and forgiven. It was a tree upon which He was nailed, not a beautiful, wooden cross that is depicted in Christian art today. The perfect blood of the Messiah is the only thing that could wash away the sin of the ages. The scene on the cross would have been much more primitive and morbid that we could imagine, but much more powerful than we can conceive. He could not die lying down; He had to be lifted up from the earth.

"His body shall not remain all night upon the tree, but thou shalt in any wise bury him that day; (for he that is hanged is accursed by God;) that thy land be not defiled, which the Lord thy God giveth thee for an inheritance." **Deut.21:23. Gal.3:13.**

"And I, if I be lifted up from the earth, will draw all men unto me." **John 12:32.**

"And as Moses lifted up the serpent in the wilderness, even so must the Son of man be lifted up." **John 3:14.**

"And we are witnesses of all things which he did both in the land of the Jews, and in Jerusalem; whom they slew and hanged on a tree." **Acts 10:39.**

During those six hours when *Yeshua* was the cross, there were several supernatural things that happened that also proved that He wasn't just another martyr dying for a good cause.

1) *Darkness cover all the land* (**Matt.27:45**)
2) *Yeshua quoted* **Psalm 22:1** *as a cry of victory, that God keeps His promises* (**Matt.27:46**)
3) *Yeshua yielded up the ghost, they did not take it* (**Matt.27:50, John 10:18**)
4) *The veil of the temple was torn in half from the top to the bottom* (**Matt.27:51, Heb.10:20**)
5) *There was an earthquake* (**Matt.27:51**)

The death of the Messiah was only the valley through which He would pass through in order to prove beyond any shadow of a doubt, that He was the long awaited Messiah. He would have to be buried! This way His people would not have to fear the grave, and they would have the assurance that their Lord would be with them. We don't have to worry about being buried in the ground, or some mausoleum, or some fancy concrete tomb, we know that our Savior has already passed through that way before us. Sometimes we forget that the burial of the Messiah was the second part of the gospel; the death, the burial, and the resurrection.

"For I delivered unto you first of all that which I also received, how that Christ died for our sins according to the scriptures; And that he was buried, and that he rose again the third day according to the scriptures." **I Cor.15:3-4.**

There was a *rich* man, named Joseph of Arimathaea, who was a secret disciple of *Yeshua*. He prepared his own tomb, hewn out of a rock, that would be used in order to fulfill the prophecy of **Isa.53:9**. Interestingly, the prophecies said that the Messiah would have His ministry primarily among the poor, **Isa.61:1, Luke 4:18,** but a rich man was used in order to fulfill the prophecies concerning His burial.

If there had been no resurrection of the Messiah, there would be no faith, no need of preaching the gospel, and no hope for those who have gone on before us, who died in faith. It would be a sad place to live, if we only had hope in the Messiah while we are alive on this earth. The risen Messiah is at the very heart of the Christian faith.

Women were chosen to be the first ones to see Him after He was resurrected. What women? The women, from Galilee, who had followed Him all the way to Jerusalem, which was about eighty miles on foot. The fact that women were chosen by the Messiah proves that the gospels are not just Jewish legends or fables, because religious Jews would have never included women in their story. We sometimes overlook these powerful women, but they are mentioned early in *Yeshua's* ministry, **Luke 8:1-3,** at the garden tomb, **Luke 24:10**, and also in the upper room waiting for the coming of the Holy Spirit, **Acts 1:14.**

Yeshua ate before the disciples to prove that He was risen, **Luke 24:39-43.** *Yeshua* didn't leave anyone out, after He appeared to the disciples on that glorious Lord's day and Thomas was not there; eight days later He appeared again, and Thomas proclaimed, *"My Lord and my God."* **John 20:28.**

Yeshua told His disciples that He would meet them back at Galilee, after He had risen, **Matt.26:32.** Why? Try to imagine meeting the crucified and risen Lord back where He had called you from the beginning? He was giving them the assurance that He was the same person who had been with them for over three years, but now risen from the dead. He made breakfast for the disciples on the shore, probably near the place where He had called them to follow Him, **John 21**.

Yeshua would take His disciples up on a mountain and give them their marching orders about going into the known world for the very first time. They were to be representatives of God's kingdom, and wherever they went, *Yeshua* would be with them through the presence of the Holy Spirit, **Matt.28:16-20**. The message of the risen Messiah would be central to the message of those first apostles.

"Whom God raised up, having loosed the pains of death: because it was not possible that he should be holden of it." **Acts 2:24.**

"Therefore let all the house of Israel know assuredly, that God hath made that same Jesus, whom ye have crucified, both Lord and Christ." **Acts 2:36.**

"And if Christ be not risen, then is our preaching vain, and your faith is also vain. Yea, and we are found false witnesses of God: because we have testified of God that he raised up Christ: whom he raised not up, if so be that the dead rise not. For if the dead rise not, then is not Christ raised: And if Christ be not raised, your faith is vain; ye are yet in your sins. Then they also which are fallen asleep in Christ are perished. If in this life only we have hope in Christ, we are of all men most miserable." **I Cor.15:14-19.**

The Biblical evidence is there, and the historical evidence is there, that *Yeshua* truly is the Messiah. So now, we must answer this question for ourselves, *"But whom say ye that I am?"*

YESHUA
THE
GOD~MAN

THE ACCURACY OF
SCRIPTURES

"For thy mercy is great unto the heavens, and thy truth unto the clouds." **Psalms 57:10.**

"Thy word is true from the beginning." **Psalm 119:160.**

"Every word of God is pure." **Proverbs 30:5.**

There has to be absolute *truth,* or the Hebrew *"emeth,"* in the universe, not everything can be relative. Some people say, *"You have your truth and I have mine."* Another person will say, *"Truth is only what we can understand with our minds".* Then there is the pragmatic person who says, *"Truth is only what works".* But the Hebrew word for truth means an *"absolute certainty",* even if some people do not believe it. Just because someone does not believe the truth does not change the fact that it is still truth. Once I was witnessing to a young man who had been discouraged about his faith, because an intellectual, atheist made him feel so ignorant. As I shared with him, I asked him, *"Do you believe in the Bible, and that Jesus was the Son of God?"* He said, *"Yes, I do, but that man made me feel so bad that I quit talking about it to anyone."* The problem was that the atheist was more educated on what he didn't believe than the young man was on what he believed. After a long conversation I saw him began to change and he thanked me for spending time with him. He just needed to know that truth is truth regardless of what others say, and even if we do not understand it. I don't understand how a monarch butterfly can hatch from an egg in south Texas, migrate to Canada, and then fly back south to one certain mountain in Mexico in the winter, and go back to Texas and start all over again. But it is the truth!

We must begin our study by affirming the reliability of the sacred scriptures. Before we can understand the importance of knowing *Yeshua* as the God-Man, it is imperative that we see the importance of being able to rely on the infallible truth of the Bible. One does not bury their head in the sand and deny the fact that there have been scribal variants over the centuries, and there are translational discrepancies in the scriptures. But there are no errors in the original, inspired Word of God! The Lord God Almighty has still preserved the body of absolute truth that is contained within the sacred scriptures. My faith is not in a translation of the Bible, but in the body of truth that it contains, and on the person of the *Yeshua* of the Bible.

INTERNAL EVIDENCE

The Bible tells us how the scriptures were written:

"For the prophecy came not in old time by the will of man: but holy men of God spake as they were moved by the Holy Ghost." **2 Peter 1:21.**

Over a period of about 1500 years, with over 40 authors, the Holy Spirit was the orchestrator of the sacred writings. The Old Testament was written from around 1400BC - 400BC. The New Testament was written from 37AD - 100AD. How could a writer from Old Testament times write down a prophecy that correlated with another writer who wrote during the first century AD? It would be like breaking a watch into thousands of pieces and dropping in the middle of the ocean, and when all of the pieces of the watch hit the bottom the watch would be back together. Impossible? Not with God! For sake of time and space I will try to give some of the reasons why it is important to know that the Bible gives us the very basis for knowing truth.

ONE GOD

We know that the sacred scriptures give us the absolute truth that there is one God Almighty and there is none other. *"In the beginning, God created the heaven and the earth."* **Gen.1:1.** *"Hear, O Israel: The Lord our God is one Lord."* **Deut.6:4.** It's interesting that two different Hebrew names, "YHVH" and "Elohim" are both in **Deut.6:4**. The Hebrew name for *"God"* in **Gen.1:1**, is *"Elohim"*, which is plural. This Hebrew name for God is used over 2500 times in the Old Testament. The Bible records many times that *"God said, ...and it was so."* What language did God speak when He created everything?

"By the word of the Lord were the heavens made; and all the host of them by the breath of his mouth." **Psalm 33:6.**

"For he spake, and it was done; he commanded, and it stood fast." **Psalm 33:9.**

Probably Hebrew! Because this was the language of *Yeshua* as we will see later.

Several times in **Gen.1**, we find that after God created everything, the Bible says, *"and God saw that it was good."* There was a mutual blessing when God created nature; God would be blessed by it, and nature would bless God in return. When God created man, He blessed them, and they were to bless God in return. This mutual blessing was lost after the fall in **Gen.3**. The coming of *Yeshua* the God-Man into the world would restore this blessing spiritually at His first coming and physically at His second coming. It is crucial that we understand God's divine purpose for creating everything. Again, God would bless creation, and creation would bless God. Creation would bless man, and man would bless creation. Man would bless his wife, and his wife would bless him. The husband and wife would bless their children and the children would bless their parents. But it was when man thought that he could be his own boss that all of the troubles started in the world. Even creation is groaning for its redemption. And this will happen at the return of *Yeshua* when He establishes His reign on the earth.

"For we know that the whole creation groaneth and travaileth in pain together until now." **Romans 8:22.**

So there is one God, but He operates in three persons. We even find the plural pronouns like *"us"* in places like **Genesis 1:26, 3:22,** and **Genesis 11:7,** and *Yeshua* used the plural pronoun *"we"* in **John 17:22.** There is a beautiful picture of the trinity at the baptism of *Yeshua*, in **Matt.3:16-17.** The Son of God is standing in the Jordan River, the Holy Spirit descends upon Him, and the Father speaks from heaven. Also, *Yeshua* gave His disciples the formula for baptism when He said, *"Go ye therefore, and teach all nations, baptizing them in the <u>name</u> of the Father, and of the Son, and of the Holy Ghost."* **Matt.28:19.** Notice the word *"name"* is singular, but there are three distinct Persons, The Father, The Son, and The Holy Ghost. The doctrine of the Triune Godhead was believed and taught by the first Jewish followers in *Yeshua*. Even though the word *"trinity"* is not in the Bible, the actions of the God of Israel presuppose three distinct Persons operating as one God. Again, we cannot fully understand this mystery, but it is clearly taught in the sacred scriptures. Early church fathers like Theophilus of Antioch, Ignatius, and Tertullian, Justyn Martyr, and others, taught this doctrine as well.

When *Elohim* started dealing with his people, his name was compounded to fit whatever the need of man was within the context. Compounded names like:

"Yehovah-Elohim" = The self- existent One who reveals Himself
"Yehovah-jireh" = The Lord will provide
"Yehovah-rapha" = The Lord that healeth
"Yehovah-nissi" = The Lord our banner
"Yehovah-Shalom" = The Lord our peace
"Yehovah-ra-ah" = The Lord my shepherd
"Yehovah-tsidkenu" = The Lord our righteousness
"Yehovah- shammah" = The Lord is present

The reason it is so important to understand these Hebrew names of God in the Old Testament is because these names would come to fruition in the person of *Yeshua* when He came to this earth. *Yeshua* revealed God, He provided righteousness, He heals us, He waves His banner of love over us, He gives us true peace, He is our Good Shepherd, and He is ever present with us because He lives within His people.

ISRAEL

We can read in the Old Testament where God raised up a nation called Israel through a man named, *Abraham*. Through this nation would come salvation to the world through the *"seed"* of Abraham that would be ultimately fulfilled in *Yeshua*. **Matt.1:1,**

"The book of the generation of Jesus Christ, the son of David, the son of Abraham." And we find these all-important words in **Galatians 3:16**:

"Now to Abraham and his seed were the promises made. He saith not, And to seeds, as of many; but as of one, And to thy seed, which is Christ."

The name *"Israel"* is first mentioned in **Gen.32:28**, when God changed Jacob's name. The name *Israel* would be used for national and spiritual *Israel*. However, I think it is needful to mention that there is a biblical difference from the *"seed of Abraham"* and the *"children of Abraham"*. The Jews who embraced *Yeshua* as their Messiah are called *"children of Abraham."*

"For they are not all Israel, which are of Israel: Neither, because they are the seed of Abraham, are they all children; but, in Isaac shall thy seed be called." **Romans 9:6b-7**

But there is no way to properly understand the scriptures without a proper understanding of the promises that God made to Israel. God's intent was to bless Israel and Israel would bless God in return, and through Israel the world would be blessed. Israel has given us the scriptures, the law, the promises, the covenants, and even more important, Israel has given us *Yeshua*.

"Who are Israelites; to whom pertaineth the adoption, and the glory, and the covenants, and the giving of the law, and the service of God, and the promises; Whose are the fathers, and of whom as concerning the flesh Christ came, who is over all, God blessed for ever. Amen. **Rom.9:4-5.**

Israel was to show the world how to live spiritually and morally, and when they failed, *Yeshua*, the Jewish Messiah, came to restore that blessing back to humanity.

"I am come that they might have life, and that they might have it more abundantly." **John 10:10b.**

And even though Israel disobeyed the Lord many times throughout their history, we find these strange words recorded:

"Thus saith the Lord, which giveth the sun for a light by day, and the ordinances of the moon and of the stars for a light by night, which divideth the sea when the waves thereof roar; The Lord of hosts is his name: If those ordinances depart from before me, saith the Lord, then the seed of Israel also shall cease from being a nation before me for ever. Thus saith the Lord; If heaven above can be measured, and the foundations of the earth searched out beneath, I will also cast off all the seed of Israel for all that they have done, saith the Lord." **Jere.31:35-37.**

Even though the nation of Israel was dispersed from their homeland for over eighteen hundred years, they are a nation today, and they are still called *"Israel."* (May 14, 1948) The fact that there is even a nation called Israel in the world today is one of the proofs that the Bible is true. The reason it is important to know about Israel, is because we can see that God made a covenant with Israel and those promises will be kept. It is a mystery, and many theologians and believers have a problem trying to make sense out of God's relationship with Israel. This has led to people over spiritualizing the verses that pertain to Israel, and try to make them apply to the church. But if God would graft the wild branches, believing Gentiles into the good olive tree (Israel), how much more shall He graft the natural branches (Israel) back into their own olive tree?

Romans 11:24. We can see God's mercy and longsuffering with Israel, and how He promised king David that His kingdom would come through his house and that kingdom would last forever.

"And thine house and thy kingdom shall be established for ever before thee: thy throne shall be established for ever." **II Sam. 7:16**

When *Yeshua* came into the world, He came to Israel, as the *"Son of David"*, **Matt.1:1.** This title was given to *Yeshua* some seventeen times in the New Testament. Israel was called a *"son"* in **Exo.4:22,** and *Yeshua* became the *"greater Son"* in **Matt.2:15,** who would obey the Father's will. Israel broke the Lord's commandments and *Yeshua* was the law personified. He came to satisfy the Father's holy justice in the universe. He was not only *born under the law,* He came to *fulfill the law.*

"But when the fullness of time was come, God sent forth his Son, made of a woman, made under the law." **Gal.4:4**

"Think not that I am come to destroy the law, or the prophets: I am not come to destroy, but to fulfill." **Matt.5:17**

His death on the tree provided forgiveness for all who have broken God's law, and that is everyone, Jew and Gentile. **Rom.3:23.** When *Yeshua* returns, He will be coming back to Israel, and His righteousness will cover the earth when He sits on the throne of his father David.

"He shall be great, and shall be called the Son of the Highest: and the Lord God shall give unto him the throne of his father David." **Luke 1:32.**

Woven throughout the written history of Israel, we find the prophecies concerning the first and second coming of Israel's Messiah, *Yeshua*. Hidden within the historical context of the nation of Israel, is a Hebrew *"remez"*, or *hint* of the coming Messiah. These are hidden, mysterious prophecies concerning the coming Messiah. Sometimes they are obvious and sometimes they are hidden within the Hebrew text. The *remez* could be hidden within the numerical value of a Hebrew word, *gematria*, or hidden as a metaphor, or by a verse having multiple meanings. There are hundreds of these *hints* throughout the Old Testament. We can read about the prophecies being fulfilled concerning His first coming in the gospel accounts, and the promise of His second coming is mentioned all through the prophets of old, and the New Testament. How could the prophet Micah write down where the Messiah was to be born hundreds of years before He came? **Micah 5:2**. How did Isaiah know to write that the Messiah would be born of a virgin? **Isa.7:14**. How did the Psalmist and the prophet Zechariah know that the Messiah would be crucified, even before crucifixion was invented? **Psalm 22, Zech.12:10**. Seeing these and hundreds of other prophecies being fulfilled in *Yeshua* is one more way of knowing that the scriptures are true. On many occasions *Yeshua* said, *"that the scriptures might be fulfilled."* There are an estimated 700 prophecies in the Bible concerning the Messiah. Over 300 of those prophecies were fulfilled in His first coming. The chances of just *one* of those prophecies being fulfilled in one person, called *Yeshua*, defies all logic. Impossible? Not with God!

THE GOSPELS

Our primary focus in this study is through the gospel accounts, *Matthew, Mark, Luke* and *John*. This cuts to the very heart of the sacred scriptures, because the person of *Yeshua* is the One that the scriptures are written *about*, and the One to whom the scriptures are pointing people to believe *in*.

"Then said I, Lo, I come: in the volume of the book it is written of me." **Psalm 40:7, Hebrews 10:7.**

The gospels were recorded when the Holy Spirit brought back to the hearts and minds of the apostles what to write down. Not everything has been recorded that *Yeshua* did or said, but the Holy Spirit has preserved the four gospels that we have today. The gospels were not intended to give us everything that *Yeshua* did, but for us to know Him in a personal way. Each one of the gospel accounts helps to complete the other three.

"But the Comforter, which is the Holy Ghost, whom the Father will send in my name, he shall teach you all things, and bring all things to your remembrance, whatsoever I have said unto you." **John 14:26.**

The primary purpose of the gospels is to show just who *Yeshua* was, and resulting in salvation to all who would believe. The Old Testament was pointing to the gospels, and the epistles are looking back to the gospels. We should not become just followers of Moses, or Elijah, or Peter, or followers of Paul, but followers of *Yeshua*. The purpose of the Holy Spirit is to glorify *Yeshua*!

"He shall glorify me." **John 16:14.**

"But these are written, that ye might believe that Jesus is the Christ, the Son of God; and that believing ye might have life through his name." **John 20:31.**

<u>Truth</u> is a major motif in the gospels, especially in the gospel of John. Here are a few examples:

"Pilate therefore said unto him, Art thou a king then? Jesus answered, Thou sayest that I am a king. To this end was I born, and for this cause came I into the world, that I should bear witness unto the truth. Every one that is of the truth heareth my voice." **John 18:37.**

"But now ye seek to kill me, a man that hath told you the truth, which I have heard of God: this did not Abraham." **John 8:40.**

"And because I tell you the truth, ye believe me not." **John 8:45.**

"Sanctify them through thy truth: thy word is truth." **John 17:17.**

"And for their sakes I sanctify myself, that they also might be sanctified through the truth." **John 17:19.**

"Howbeit when he, the Spirit of truth is come, he will guide you into all truth: for he shall not speak of himself; but whatsoever he shall hear, that shall he speak: and he will shew you things to come." **John 16:13.**

"This is the disciple which testifieth of these things, and wrote these things: and we know that his testimony is true." **John 21:14.**

Yeshua was more than just a philosophical concept, He embodied truth. *Yeshua* did not come to just rightly interpret the law, He was the law personified.

"And the Word was made flesh, and dwelt among us, (and we beheld his glory, the glory as of the only begotten of the Father,) full of grace and truth." **John 1:14.**

"For the law was given by Moses, but grace and truth came by Jesus Christ." **John 1:17.**

"And ye shall know the truth, and the truth shall make you free." **John 8:32.**

Yeshua even said that He was the truth. Wow!

"Jesus saith unto him, I am the way, the truth, and the life: no man cometh unto the Father, but by me." **John 14:6.**

We know that there is a heaven because *Yeshua* told us so. Absolute certainty! The Hebrew word for *"faith"* is *"emunah"*, and it means, *"security"*.

"In my Father's house are many mansions: if it were not so, I would have told you, I go to prepare a place for you." **John 14:2.**

B'RIT CHADASHAH

The New Testament, or the *B'rit Chadashah*, is comprised of the four gospels, the story of the first church and how Christianity spread in the early first century, by reading Acts and the Epistles. The Book of the Revelation is the revelation of the glorified *Yeshua*, the Aleph and the Tav, the Beginning and the End, showing us that all of history will close one day as a result of the sinful curse that has been on the earth. The curtain will close someday, and we can easily see that the time is drawing near. That curse will be lifted when *Yeshua* returns in clouds of glory, and all evil will be punished. The blessing will be restored once for all, and the devil and his followers will be done away with forever.

The books of the New Testament were written primarily by people who walked with *Yeshua* when He walked this earth. They were first-hand, eyewitnesses of His ministry, His death, His resurrection, and His ascension. It is one thing to repeat what someone has said and write it down in a book, it is quite another thing to record what you have seen with your eyes and heard with your ears, and have felt in your own heart. So they were eyewitnesses of the truth. The Bible cannot be compared to religious books; it is based on absolute truth. The power of the written Word of God has changed countless lives over the centuries. For example; most of the orthodox, religious Jews, do not read the New Testament, and they do allow their children to read it. But many of them have come to faith in *Yeshua*, as their Messiah, once they read the New Testament for themselves. As one dear Jewish friend of mine said; *"Once I read the Brit Chadashah for myself, I saw that Yeshua was the one that the prophets wrote about, and I became a believer."* The words of the New Testament are not just words, they are life! *Yeshua* said:

"the words I speak unto you, they are spirit, and they are life." **John 6:63.**

"That which was from the beginning, which we have heard, which we have seen with our eyes, which we have looked upon, and our hands have handled, of the Word of life; (For the life was manifested, and we have seen it, and bear witness, and shew unto you that eternal life, which was with the Father, and was manifested unto us;) **I John 1:1-2.**

OUTSIDE EVIDENCE

Over the centuries, there has not been found one historical proof that disproves the sacred scriptures. History, geography, archaeology, astronomy, and science all prove the Bible is true. For example; not only is there still a nation called *"Israel"*, but many of the cities and towns are still called by the same names that were recorded in the Bible. There still is a city called Jerusalem, a city called Bethlehem, a city called Nazareth, a village called Capernaum, a city called Tiberius, a city called Caesarea, a city called Jericho, a village called Bethany, pools called Bethesda and Siloam, a real Garden of Gethsemane, a real Mt. of Olives, a real Jordan River, and a real Sea of Galilee. Proper names in the Bible were real people and real places. Archaeologists have found innumerable coins, pottery, tablets, statues, building stones, and ancient writings that put validity to the scriptures. Many finds have the names written of kings, leaders, and various people that are mentioned in the Bible. There really were actual, historical people like, Caesar Augustus, Herod the Great, Pontius Pilate, Tiberius Caesar, who lived during the birth, the ministry, the death and resurrection of *Yeshua*. Ossuaries have been discovered on the Mt. of Olives from *Yeshua's* time, that have the names of many of the people in the New Testament. Burial boxes with the names of people like: *Marta* (Martha), *Miriam* (Mary), *Eleazar*, (Lazarus), *Shappira* (Sapphira), *Joseph son of Caiaphas*, and hundreds more.

There is outside evidence that the Old Testament stories are true. There is strong evidence that the dramatic account of the *Exodus* has been located, but not in the Sinai Peninsula, where most people have been looking all of these years. The Bible says on several occasions that God took Moses and the children of Israel *"out of Egypt"*. Marine biologists have discovered where the children of Israel crossed over the Red Sea, in present-day, Gulf of Aqaba. In 1984, the original *Mt. Sinai* was discovered in present-day Saudi Arabia, (the Bible land of *Midian,* **Exo.3:1**) and the mountain is called *Jabal El Lawz*. (**Read Galatians 4:25**) The stones at the top of the mountain are all black, where they have been burned in a tremendous fire. **Exo.19:18**. A few years later, another team of archaeologists traveled to Saudi Arabia and confirmed this finding, along with testimonies from many of the local Bedouins who lived there. They also found the bitter waters of *Marah,* **Exo.15:23,** the caves of *Moses,* (with carvings on the inside of the caves about *Moses*). The twelve wells of water at *Elim,* **Exo.15:27,** and the altar where they built the golden calf, **Exo.32:1-6,** where they also found petroglyph carvings of cows on the sides of the altar.

Many archaeologists believe that *Noah's* ark has been discovered on *Mt. Ararat* in present-day Turkey. Archaeologists have found the place of *Sodom and Gomorrah,* the walls of *Jericho,* and the house of *king David,* and cities built by the *Hittites.* Over 25,000 sites have been discovered that authenticate that the Bible is true, and nothing has been found that disproves the Bible. The sacred scriptures do not contain legends or myths, or allegories, they are real!

HISTORY

There is evidence among historians during the first and second centuries after *Yeshua.* We even find secular historians like Josephus, Phlegon, Tacitus, Thallus, Marcrobius, Suetonius, Pliny the Younger, Lucian, and others, referring to *Yeshua* as *"Christ, or Christus",* in their writings. Even the Babylonian Talmud mentions *"Yeshu the Nazarene,"* which is a corrupt form of the name *Yeshua.* While it sounds and looks very similar, the unbelieving Jews called his name *"Yeshu",* which means *"may his name be blotted out."* But almost every one mentions the crucifixion of *Yeshua,* and the faith of his followers. It is also helpful to study the writings of people like Jerome, Eusebius, Epiphinius, Tertullian, Clement of Alexandria, Irenaeus, and others. The apostle John lived until about 102AD, and his writings are documented by Prochorus, one of the seven deacons, **Acts 6:5,** He was put on the Island of Patmos with John, during the reign of Domitian, the Roman emperor.

CREATION

Creation is convincing evidence that the Bible is true. Think of the universe and the power of God that holds everything together. Look at the planets, the stars, and the solar system. Study the constellations of the stars and the galaxies, mentioned in **Job 38:31-32**, and try to imagine that God is so big that He knows every star by name. **Psalm 147:4, Isa.40:26**. God has even properly measured the balance of the earth and knows every bucket of water in the ocean. **Isa.40:12**. What about the moisture in the clouds that provides rain, mentioned in **Job 38:25-28, Psalm 147:8**. The weather patterns, the wind, the dawning of a new day, the night, the flowers, the birds, and all we can say is "Wow"! The earth is tilted 23°, and if it was tilted any more or any less, the water would flood the land. If the earth was any closer to the burning inferno, called the sun, the people on planet earth would burn up. If the earth was any farther away from the sun, the people on planet earth would freeze to death. God is greater than any finite mind can understand, and if we could understand Him, then He would not be God.

"The heavens declare the glory of God; and the firmament sheweth his handywork. Day unto day uttereth speech, and night unto night sheweth knowledge. There is no speech nor language, where their voice is not heard." **Psalm 19:1-3.**

"For the invisible things of him from the creation of the world are clearly seen, being understood by the things that are made, even his eternal power and Godhead; so that they are without excuse." **Rom.1:20.**

Have you ever contemplated the human body? The arteries and veins in one human body could stretch around the entire world.

Think about the five senses that we have; seeing, feeling, hearing, smelling, and tasting. *Yeshua* had deep compassion on anyone who had lost one or more of their senses, because they can be used as a way of expression of our love to God. Think of the generations who have lived and died before us, and why were we born during this time? Think of the joy and the innocence of a child. While we are not plugged into an electrical socket, our heart is constantly pumping blood all through our bodies. We have the ability to love, to hate, to think, to sleep, to work, to eat, to walk upright, the health to work and enjoy the fruits of our labor. No wonder the psalmist said:

"I will praise thee; for I am fearfully and wonderfully made: marvelous are thy works; and that my soul knoweth right well." **Psalm 139:14.**

CHANGED LIVES

But probably the greatest evidence outside of the Bible that proves that the scriptures are true; is a *changed life!* Countless sinners have found forgiveness and the power to completely turn from their sins through faith in *Yeshua.* **2 Cor.5:17.** Think about all of the millions of people down through the centuries who have found purpose for their lives in *Yeshua.* The peace, the joy, the comfort, the purpose, the love that filled their lives, their courage to face death, can only be explained by the supernatural power of the risen *Yeshua.* Though we cannot explain how God changes our lives, we can say as the healed blind man in **John 9:25,** *"one thing I know, that, whereas I was blind, now I see."*

How was the message of *Yeshua* able to overcome the Roman empire, the corrupt Jewish establishment, and conquer the known world? It was through the power that changed the lives of those who truly believed in Him. What would cause a follower of *Yeshua* to give his or her life for the gospel? It was the fact that they knew it to be absolute truth! One will not die for something that they know to be a lie, but they will die for something they know to be the truth. Concerning the persecutions that the first century believers in *Yeshua* encountered, here is a quote from Cornelius Tacitus, a pagan, Roman historian who lived from 56-120AD.

"Consequently, to get rid of the report, Nero fastened the guilt and inflicted the most exquisite tortures on a class hated for their abominations, called Christians by the populace. Christus, from whom the name had its origin, suffered the extreme penalty during the reign of Tiberius at the hands of one of our procurators, Pontius Pilatus, and a most mischievous superstition, thus checked for the moment, again broke out not only in Judaea, the first source of evil, but even in Rome, where all things hideous and shameful from every part of the world find their centre and become popular. Accordingly, an arrest was first made of all who pleaded guilty; then, upon their information, an immense multitude was convicted, not so much of the crime of firing the city, as of hatred against mankind. Mockery of every sort was added to their deaths. Covered with the skins of beasts, they were torn by dogs and perished, or were nailed to crosses, or were doomed to the flames and burnt, to serve as a nightly illumination, when daylight had expired."

–*Annals 14.44*

Conclusion

1. Christ lived during the reign of Tiberius Caesar
2. Pontius Pilate put him to death
3. The word "superstition" suggests a religion
4. Christ had followers who were named Christians
5. Christians suffered under Nero and they were hated by others

THINKING HEBRAICALLY

Since Hebrew was the original language of the Old Testament, before it was translated into the Greek Septuagint in the 3rd century BC, and the language that *Yeshua* spoke was Hebrew in **Acts 26:14**, this tells us that we need to think Hebraically when we study about our Lord. *Yeshua* did not speak Greek, or Latin, or English, or German, He spoke Hebrew. *Yeshua* taught himself by using the Hebrew *Tanakh* .

"And beginning at Moses and all the prophets, he expounded unto them in all the scriptures the things concerning himself. **Luke 24:27**

"And he said unto them, These are the words which I spake unto you, while I was yet with you, that all things must be fulfilled, which were written in the law of Moses, and in the prophets, and in the psalms, concerning me." **Luke 24:44**

Even though the gospel narratives that are recorded in Mark, Luke, and John, were written in Greek, they were Hebrew in thought. Matthew was first written in Hebrew and later translated into Greek. This has been a missing link in western world Christianity. We have spent too much time studying the language that was used to communicate the gospels, instead of their original thought.

The late pastor, and Hebrew scholar, Robert Lindsay, who pastored a Southern Baptist church in Jerusalem, discovered back in the 1950's that the gospels were Hebrew in their origination. After years of research, along with Hebrew scholar, David Flusser, they found more and more proof through the style of the sentences, and the phrasing, the customs, and the Hebrew semitisms, that the gospels were Hebraic, not Greek in thought. Many colleges today still argue this point and teach the gospels from a Greek, philosophical perspective. This has caused millions of well-intended Christians and Bible teachers to miss a world of knowledge about our Lord.

The death, burial, and resurrection of *Yeshua* fulfilled the Jewish feasts of Passover, Unleavened Bread, and Firstfruits. Again, these were Jewish feasts, not Greek. When *Yeshua* attended the Feast of Tabernacles in **John 7:2**, it was a Jewish feast not a Greek feast. When *Yeshua* was in Jerusalem during the Feast of Dedication or Feast of Hanukkah, in **John 10:22**, that was a Jewish feast not a Greek feast. The Samaritan woman noticed quickly that *Yeshua* was a Jew in **John 4:9**. John's gospel was penned in Greek in the latter part of the first century, but he was communicating the message of the Hebrew *Yeshua* to a Greek-speaking audience. There are numerous Aramaic/Hebrew words still in the English translation of the New Testament. Aramaic was spoken among the village people in Galilee, and was a dialect of Hebrew. Here are a few of them, thus also showing that the gospels have a Hebrew origination.

"Raca" = *"empty headed, or fool"* **Matthew 5:22.**

"mammon" = *"money"* **Matthew 6:24, Luke 16:9.**

"Talitha cumi" = *"Damsel, arise"* **Mark 5:41.**

"Ephphatha" = *"be opened"* **Mark 7:34.**

"Corban" = *"a gift"* **Mark 7:11.**

"Eli, Eli, lama sabachthani" = *"My God, my God, why hast thou forsaken me"* **Matthew 27:46, Psalm 22:1.**

"Rabboni" = *"My Master"* **John 20:16.**

When we think Hebraically, we interpret the gospel accounts from the Jewish perspective, because *Yeshua* was a Jew, who came for the lost sheep of the house of Israel. **Matt. 10:6,15:24.** He was offering the kingdom to Israel. How did the words of *Yeshua* connect to what the prophets said? What was the religious, political, and geographical background to the passage of scripture? What were some of the traditional and customary mindsets of His day? What were the messianic expectations of the early first century? Why did *Yeshua* make His hometown in Capernaum? How radical was it for *Yeshua* to take His disciples across the lake, into the land of the Decapolis? Without the proper understanding of the context, we will make the scriptures say something totally different than what they were written to say. Once we understand the context, then the Holy Spirit will speak to us with the proper, moral application. This is called a *"midrash"* in Hebrew thought. Give the scriptures their proper, contextual intent, and the Holy Spirit will touch each person differently, according to where they are in their spiritual life.

This has been one of the biggest problems over the centuries among theologians and Bible students. The message of *Yeshua* was communicated to the Roman world primarily in the common language of the empire, which was Greek. But when we study the Jewish scriptures only from the Greek perspective, we are missing a goldmine of understanding. I'm not trying to discourage anyone from studying Greek, but the only way to properly connect the Old Testament and *Yeshua* is from the Hebrew mind. He was a Jewish Messiah who came to His chosen people, Israel, and Hebrew was the language of the religious Jew in the early first century. It was a tri-lingual society, and Hebrew was still a very active language among the religious Jews.

"And a superscription also was written over him in letters of Greek, and Latin, and Hebrew, THIS IS THE KING OF THE JEWS." **Luke 23:38.**

The majority of the Roman, Hellenized *(to make one form to the Greek culture)* world spoke Greek. The Romans spoke Latin, and the religious Jews spoke Hebrew. The gospel of *Yeshua* was taught first from the Hebrew perspective, received first by Jewish followers, before the message was later received by other people in the Roman world. **Acts 2:5, 8-11.** We believe that when the Latin-speaking Cornelius in **Acts 10:1**, received the Holy Spirit, he spoke in the Hebrew tongue, as a confirmation to the Jewish Peter that he was truly saved without having to keep the law of Moses. This was a major turning point in Christianity. It was very necessary for the gospel to be translated in other languages as it spread into the known world. I'm so thankful that the gospel was translated into English, so I could hear the message and believe the gospel. But when we are trying to understand who our Savior really was, He must be understood from Hebrew thought. *Yeshua* did not speak English! I still go into some churches today where the pastor gets offended if I do not use the English, King James Version of the Bible. Which I always do anyway, but it's sad that they are still focusing on a translation of the Bible, instead of the *Yeshua* of the Bible. There was not even an English word for every Hebrew word in the year 1611AD.

When we have a proper Hebrew understanding of the one true God of the Old Testament, then we can better understand who *Yeshua* was. Many of the problems that our churches have faced in the western worldview has been brought on by studying the scriptures from a Greek, philosophical mind. There is a tremendous breakdown when it comes to the relationship of *Yeshua* and God when one studies from the Greek perspective. This was foreign to the Jewish mind, and foreign to the way the first followers of *Yeshua* believed and worshipped. Simply put, the God of the Old Testament was defined as being the Creator and His relationship with Israel. God proved who He was by what He did. From the Greek perspective, the God of the Bible is only defined by the intellectual and philosophical analysis. But the authors of the gospel narratives were Jews, not Greeks. They describe *Yeshua* as being the true Messiah by His deeds, not just by their reasoning. When we turn into the pages of the gospels, we see *Yeshua* proving that He was the God of the Old Testament by how He was born, His ministry, His death, His resurrection, and His ascension. One good example of thinking Hebraically, is when *Yeshua* gave this answer to John the Baptist when John was in prison, and asked was *Yeshua* the Messiah or should they look for another?

"The blind receive their sight, and the lame walk, the lepers are cleansed, and the deaf hear, the dead are raised up, and the poor have the gospel preached to them." **Matthew 11:5.**

"If I do not the works of my Father, believe me not. But if I do, though ye believe not me, believe the works: that ye may know, and believe, that the Father is in me, and I in him." **John 10:37-38.**

The works proved that He was Israel's long-awaited Messiah. When we try to interpret *Yeshua* from a Greek mind, we will end up twisting the scriptures around in order to try to prove our point, and then we will still be disappointed. Our Christian heritage did not begin in Athens or Rome, but it began in Israel. The roots of the Christian faith are Jewish, not Baptist, Methodist, Pentecostal, Church of Christ, Presbyterian, Episcopal, Puritan, Lutheran, or Catholic, or any other of the over two hundred thousand denominations. We must seek to know *Yeshua* from the pages of the sacred scriptures, not with some presupposition that we already know Him from the way we have been raised or taught as a child. This will never satisfy the majority of the world, because most people operate out of pure logic. Hebrew thought is satisfied with the *mystery* of it all. The goal of knowing *Yeshua* is worship, not to just satisfy our intellect. Even though we can know God through faith in *Yeshua*, we will never be able to comprehend all there is to know about the God of the Bible; this is thinking Hebraically.

*"The <u>secret</u> (Hebrew = **cathar**) things belong unto the Lord our God."* **Deut.29:29.**

"Who hath directed the Spirit of the Lord, or being his counsellor hath taught him?" **Isaiah 40:13.**

"For my thoughts are not your thoughts, neither are your ways my ways, saith the Lord." **Isaiah 55:7.**

*"It is the glory of God to <u>conceal</u> (Hebrew = **cathar**) a thing."* **Proverbs 25:2.**

"O the depth of the riches both of the wisdom and knowledge of God! how unsearchable are his judgments, and his ways past finding out! **Romans 11:33.**

YESHUA AS GOD

CREATOR

Yeshua is called the Creator in the Bible. He is the Son of God, the second Person of the Trinity, who was there in the beginning. Keep in mind, that there is one God who operates in three Persons.

"Who hath ascended up into heaven, or descended? who hath gathered the wind in his fists? who hath bound the waters in a garment? who hath established all the ends of the earth? what is his name, and what is his son's name, if thou canst tell?" **Proverbs 30:4.**

Notice that the Creator has a Son, and His name is mysterious.

"His name shall endure for ever: his name shall be continued as long as the sun: and men shall be blessed in him: all nations shall call him blessed." **Psalm 72:17. (The Son will continue His Father's name)**

This is a good time to emphasize the importance of *Yeshua's* name. It originated in **Numbers 13:16b**, *"And Moses called Oshea the son of Nun Jehoshua, or Yehoshuah"*. There is no "J" in Hebrew. Part of the transliterated tetragrammaton for God's name in Hebrew is *YHVH*, are pronounced in *"Yehoshuah."* When the vowels were added to *YHVH* by the scribal Masoretes, (Jewish scribes between

5-10 century AD) it was pronounced *"Yahweh"*. The meaning of "Yehoshuah" is *"Yahweh saves, or Yahweh is salvation"*. The name of the Messiah would continue on the Father's name. A shortened form of "Yehoshuah" was *"Yeshua"*, which we can find in **Nehemiah 8:17**, as a form of Joshua the son of Nun's real name. So the name *"Yeshua"* was used hundreds of years before *Yeshua* was ever born. One might ask, "Where did we get the name *"Jesus?"* Or where did we get the name, *"Jesus Christ?"* Jesus comes from the Greek *"Iesous"*, and *"Christ"* comes from the Greek word for anointed, which is *"Christos."* But the original Hebrew name for our Savior is, *"Yeshua Ha Mashiach"*. As we continue to focus on *Yeshua* being the Creator, let these holy and mysterious words sink into your ears.

"In the beginning was the Word, (**"and God <u>said</u>"** in Gen.1) *and the Word was with God, and the Word was God. The same was in the beginning with God.* **John 1:1-2.**

"And the Word (**"and God <u>said</u>"** from Gen.1) *was made flesh, and dwelt among us, (and we beheld his glory, the glory as of the only begotten of the Father,) full of grace and truth."* **John 1:14.**

"<u>All things were made by him</u> (**Yeshua**)*; and without him* (**Yeshua**) *was not any thing made that was made."* **John 1:3.**

"He (**Yeshua**) *was in the world, and <u>the world was made by him</u>* (**Yeshua**)*, and the world knew him* (**Yeshua**) *not."* **John 1:10.**

"And now, O Father, glorify thou me with thine own self with the glory which <u>I had with thee before the world was</u>." **John 17:5. (notice that Yeshua was with the Father before creation)**

114

"But to us there is but one God, the Father, of whom are all things, and we in him; and one Lord Jesus Christ, <u>by whom are all things,</u> and we by him." **I Corinthians 8:6.**

"Who is the image of the invisible God, the firstborn of every creature. <u>For by him</u> **(Yeshua)** *<u>were all things created,</u> that are in heaven, and that are in earth, visible and invisible, whether they be thrones, or dominions, or principalities, or powers: <u>all things were created by him,</u>* **(Yeshua)** *and for him* **(Yeshua).**" **Colossians 1:15-16.**

"Hath in these last days spoken unto us by his Son, **(Yeshua)** *whom he hath appointed heir of all things, <u>by whom also he made the worlds.</u>"* **Hebrews 1:2.**

"And to make all men see what is the fellowship of the mystery, which from the beginning of the world hath been hid in God, <u>who created all things by Jesus Christ.</u>" **Ephesians 3:9.**

"And have put on the new man, which is renewed in knowledge after the image of him **(Yeshua)** *<u>that created him.</u>"* **Colossians 3:10.**

"<u>I</u> **(Yeshua)** *<u>am Alpha and Omega,</u>* **(in Hebrew, the Aleph and Tav is placed together as a grammatical Hebrew style, over 11,000 times in the Bible)** *the beginning and the ending, saith the Lord, which is, and which was, and which is to come, <u>the Almighty.</u>"* **Rev.1:8.**

"And unto the angel of the church of the Laodiceans write: These things saith the Amen, the faithful and true witness, <u>the beginning of the creation of God.</u>" **Rev.3:14.**

"And he (Yeshua) was clothed with a vesture dipped in blood: and his name is called <u>the Word of God</u>." **Rev.19:13. (this connects Yeshua back to Gen.1 and John 1)**

Seeing *Yeshua* as the Creator deepens our understanding of the mystery of the incarnation. There never was a time when *Yeshua* was not. The Bible presupposes that *Yeshua* has always existed. There are many *"theophanies"* in the Old Testament where He appears as *"an angel of the Lord"*, or *"a captain of the Lord"*. **Gen.18, Exo.3, Josh. 5.** He was not created by God, He is God!

GOD IN HIS BIRTH

The holy Bible declares that *Yeshua* was God at His birth. The eternal God stepped into time in the form of a Man. Even from Old Testament times the inspired writers of the Bible knew that the coming Messiah would be none other than God Himself! The prophet Isaiah, whose name in Hebrew, *"Yeshahahu"*, means, *"Yah has saved"*, wrote more about the salvation that *Yeshua* would bring. Notice in this next verse how the coming Messiah would be a *child* and a *son*, but He would also be *God*.

"For unto us a child is born, unto us a son is given: and the government shall be upon his shoulder: and his name shall be called Wonderful, Counsellor, <u>The mighty God</u>, <u>The everlasting Father</u>, The Prince of Peace." **Isa.9:6.**

"Therefore the Lord himself shall give you a sign; Behold, a virgin shall conceive, and bear a son, and shall call his name <u>Immanuel</u>." **Isa.7:14, Matt.1:23.**

The Hebrew, transliterated word, *"Immanuel"*, means, *"with us is God."*

"But thou, Beth-lehem Ephratah, though thou be little among the thousands of Judah, yet out of thee shall he come forth unto me that is to be ruler in Israel; whose goings forth have been from old, from everlasting." **Micah 5:2, Matt.2:6.**

The Hebrew word in this verse for *"everlasting"* is *"olam."* It means, *"eternity, world without end, always."* So when we put Isaiah's prophecy together with Micah's prophecy, we see the coming Messiah will be a *"child"*, born in Bethlehem; but the *"Son"* would be from everlasting.

"Saying, Where is he that is born King of the Jews? for we have seen his star in the east, and are come to worship him." **Matt.2:2.**

"And when they were come into the house, they saw the young child with Mary his mother, and fell down, and worshipped him: and when they had opened their treasures, they presented unto him gifts; gold, frankincense, and myrrh." **Matt.2:11.**

Notice that the wise men saw the star of *Yeshua*, which connects Him to the prophecy where He is called *"A Star out of Jacob."* **Numbers 24:17.** The wise men came to worship *Yeshua*, even while He was a young child. This further shows that *Yeshua* was God at His birth. Only God receives worship!

When we come to the gospel of John, we find something very strange and yet so powerful. John could have easily used the name *"Yeshua"* when describing the incarnation, but instead John used the idea of the *"Word"* or *"logos"* becoming flesh. Because John's gospel was penned in Greek, in order to communicate the message in the latter part of the first century, most scholars say that John was using the Greek philosophical idea. But the Greek idea, *"logos,"* is only connected to man's reasoning and intellect; while the Hebrew *"memra,"* which means, *"to command,"* is connected to a divinely ordained revelation of God. I believe John was using the Hebrew thought of the *"memra"*, which was active in creation. *"And God said, …and it was so."* **Gen.1**. John would have been influenced by the Hebrew thought of *Yeshua* before he would have been influenced by the Greco-Roman world thought. Greek thought had no idea of the *"logos"* having to be *"received or rejected"*. But John's gospel says that only those who *"received"* him, or the *Word Yeshua*, would become children of God. **John 1:11-12.**

The Jewish sages wanted to distance God from any kind of human description, such as eyes, ears, nose, hands, etc., so they just used the *"memra"*, or *"command"* of God as the intermediary between God and the world. So at the very beginning of John's gospel, he takes us back to the beginning of the Bible where the *Word* was used in creation. John parallels the opening words of the book of Genesis with his gospel and also his first epistle. **I John 1:1-2.** John's gospel is different from the synoptic gospels when he talks about the incarnation. Instead of talking about the nativity setting like Matthew or Luke, which are breathtaking within themselves, John describes the coming of the Messiah into the world in this way:

*"In the beginning was the <u>Word</u>, (**Yeshua**) and the <u>Word</u> (**Yeshua**) was with God, and the <u>Word</u> (**Yeshua**) was God. The same was in the beginning with God."* **John 1:1-2.**

*"And the <u>Word</u> (**Yeshua**) was made flesh, and dwelt among us, (and we beheld his glory, the glory as of the only begotten of the Father,) full of grace and truth."* **John 1:14.**

The Word becomes something that He was not previously. The Hebrew word *"shakan"*, "to dwell" comes from the root word for *"tent"*, *"mishkan."* The Hebrew term *"skekinah"* for *"the glory of God,"* which was used for God's glory hovering over the Tabernacle, works perfectly with John's pericope. *Yeshua* was the glory of God in human flesh. When we remember that God's glory had departed from the temple in Ezekiel's day, **Eze.11:22-25**, it had been several hundred years since God's glory had been seen or heard. But when the historical time was fulfilled, **Gal.4:4**, God's glory came back to Israel in the form of *Yeshua*. But this time God's glory was not seen in a structure, or limited to a certain place, but in the *"only begotten of the Father."* *Yeshua* brought His glory to this earth, but because of His humanity, that glory was not equal to the glory that He had with the Father before the world was, that glory would return to Him after His resurrection and ascension. **John 17:5.**

The Jewish sages believed that the original Hebrew scriptures contained grace and truth. *Yeshua* was the embodiment of grace and truth.

"For the law was given by Moses, but grace and truth came by Jesus Christ.(**Yeshua Ha Mashiach**)*"* **John 1:17.**

Yeshua brings people into God's family by revealing the Father and by proving God's love for humanity. The Torah, the Word of the Lord, and the Wisdom of God were made alive in *Yeshua!* This is beyond the human mind to comprehend; it must be received by faith. The very Word of God was personified! The Almighty God, who dwells in eternity, intersected with time. The unapproachable, unknowable, omnipotent, eternal God became Man.

GOD IN HIS MINISTRY

The four gospel accounts were not designed to give us a complete biography of *Yeshua,* but were given as a perfect revelation of who He was. Just maybe, that one reason we are not given a biography of *Yeshua,* is because we would be too preoccupied with the humanity side of *Yeshua.* We must approach the gospel without having any presuppositions or theological concepts; this has caused many errors in church thought down through the centuries. It is important for us to understand that the gospels were written following the death and resurrection of *Yeshua.* They were not written as the events took place, but were written from the vantage point of the story having already been completed. So we need to be reminded that the inspired, gospel writers are giving us what was revealed to them, and later written down after all the events had transpired. They first saw *Yeshua* as only a preacher from Nazareth, but after walking with Him for over three years, and hearing His sermons, and seeing His miracles, and then witnessing His cross and resurrection and ascension, they knew beyond a shadow of a doubt that *Yeshua* was the Son of God. The term *"Son of God," "Ben Elohim,"* is used some forty three times in the New Testament. This Father/Son language goes back to the Davidic kingship of *Yeshua.* The Davidic king would have a unique relationship with God as His *"son".* The roots of Christology in the New Testament are found in the covenant that God made with David in the Old Testament.

"He shall build an house for my name, and I will stablish the throne of his kingdom for ever. I will be his father, and he shall be my son."
II Sam.7:13-14.

"I will declare the decree: the Lord hath said unto me, <u>Thou art my Son</u>; this day have I begotten thee." **Psalm 2:7.**

"He shall cry unto me, Thou art my father, my God, and the rock of my salvation. Also I will make him my <u>firstborn</u>, higher than the kings of the earth." **Psalm 89:26-27.**

This helps us to better understand the words of *Yeshua*. Notice the usage of the words *"Lord"* and *"Son"*. What sounds a little confusing at first glance, turns out to show that the *"Son of David"* is none other than the *"Lord"* himself!

"While the Pharisees were gathered together, Jesus asked them, saying, what think ye of Christ? Whose <u>son</u> is he? They say unto him, The <u>Son</u> of David. He saith unto them, How then doth David in spirit call him <u>Lord</u>, saying, The Lord **(Yehovah)** *said unto my <u>Lord</u>* **(Adonai,)***, Sit thou on my right hand, till I make thine enemies thy footstool? If David then call him <u>Lord</u>, how is he his <u>son</u>?"* **Matt.22:41-45.**

The God of the Old Testament will have a *"Son"*, *Yeshua*, who will carry on His Father's name, *Yahweh*, and *Yeshua* will have spiritual descendants who will carry on His name throughout all generations. The gospel is *His* gospel, and the gospel carries *His* name. **Acts 4:12, 9:15.** We who are called *"Christians"* are carrying on His name even to this day.

It's very interesting that while we have many instances of where *Yeshua* is called the *"Son of God"* in the gospels among his followers, we also have instances where He is called the *"Son of God"* by His enemies; by Satan, by demons, by the high priest, and those who taunted him while He was on the cross.

"And when the tempter came to him, he said, If thou be the <u>Son of God</u>, command that these stones be made bread." **Matt.4:3.**

"And unclean spirits, when they saw him, fell down before him, and cried, saying, Thou art the <u>Son of God</u>." **Mark 3:11.**

"But Jesus held his peace. And the high priest answered and said unto him, I adjure thee by the living God, that thou tell us whether thou be the Christ, the Son of God." **Matt.26:63.**

"And saying, Thou that destroyest the temple, and buildest it in three days, save thyself. If thou be the Son of God, come down from the cross." **Matt.27:40.**

"The Jews answered him, saying, For a good work we stone thee not; but for blasphemy; and because that thou, being a man, makest thyself God." **John 10:33.**

There are several times in the gospels where it is recorded that *Yeshua* was God, even from His own words.

"Jesus said unto them, Verily, verily, I say unto you, Before Abraham was, <u>I am</u>." **John 8:58. (Compare Exodus 3:14)**

"I and my Father are one." **John 10:30. (Compare Isaiah 5:2, 9:6)**

"Jesus saith unto him, Have I been so long time with you, and yet hast thou not known me, Philip? <u>he that hath seen me hath seen the Father</u>; and how sayest thou then, shew us the Father?" **John 14:9, (Compare John 1:1, 10, 14)**

"Jesus therefore, knowing all things that should come upon him, went forth, and said unto them, whom seek ye? They answered him, Jesus

of Nazareth. *Jesus saith unto them, I am he."* **John 18:4-5. (The word "he" is not in the original, so *Yeshua* was saying *"I am"*)**

There are many accounts where the divinity of *Yeshua* is mentioned. Here is one that is seldom considered. That *Yeshua* proclaimed that He was the one who sent the prophets.

"Wherefore, behold, I send unto you prophets, and wise men, and scribes." **Matt.23:34.**

While *Yeshua* walked this earth, He even mentions in His prayer to the Father about His preexistence.

"And now, O Father, glorify thou me with thine own self with the glory which I had with thee before the world was." **John 17:5.**

"Father, I will that they also, whom thou hast given me, be with me where I am; that they may behold my glory, which thou hast given me: for thou lovedst me before the foundation of the world." **John 17:24.**

Judgment will be given by *Yeshua*, and it will be based on confessing Him or denying Him.

"Whosoever therefore shall confess me before men, him will I confess also before my Father which is in heaven. But whosoever shall deny me before men, him will I also deny before my Father which is in heaven." **Matt.10:32-33.**

We read in the gospels where angels were servants to *Yeshua*, and they were His army, and the angels will accompany Him when He returns to this earth.

"Then the devil leaveth him, and, behold, angels came and ministered unto him." **Matt.4:11.**

"Thinkest thou that I cannot now pray to my Father, and he shall presently give me more than twelve legions of angels?" **Matt.26:53.**

"When the Son of man shall come in his glory, and all the holy angels with him, then shall he sit upon the throne of his glory." **Matt.25:31.**

Yeshua plainly said that He was greater than the temple, the sabbath, the prophets, or Solomon, and even Moses.

"But I say unto you, That in this place is one greater than the temple." **Matt.12:6.**

"For the Son of man is Lord even of the sabbath day." **Matt.12:8.**

"and, behold, a greater than Jonas in here." **Matt.12:41.**

"and, behold, a greater than Solomon is here." **Matt.12:42.**

"For had ye believed Moses, ye would have believed me: for he wrote of me." **John 5:46.**

"And, behold, there appeared unto them Moses and Elias talking with him." **Matt.17:3.**

"And I give unto them eternal life and they shall never perish, neither shall any man pluck them out of my hand." **John 10:28.**

Yeshua even said that He is the one who gives eternal life, and He is the one who promises that we shall never perish!

"And no man hath ascended up to heaven, but he that came down from heaven, even the Son of man which is in heaven." **John 3:13.**

"For where two or three are gathered together in my name, there am I in the midst of them." **Matthew 18:20.**

"I am with you always, even unto the end of the world." **Matthew 28:20.**

Yeshua asserted His omnipresence, stating that He had been in heaven, and was now on the earth. He would be wherever His children gathered together, and He would be with the disciples wherever they preached the gospel.

"These things said he: and after that he saith unto them, Our friend Lazarus sleepeth; and I go, that I may awake him out of sleep." **John 11:11.**

Yeshua asserted His omniscience, knowing that Lazarus had died in Bethany, near Jerusalem, and He was miles away in the desert beyond Jericho.

"All power is given unto me in heaven and in earth." **Matthew 28:18.**

Yeshua asserted His omnipotence over all creation.

The people had never heard anyone preach with the authority of *Yeshua*. It was the common practice in the early first century, to here one rabbi repeating what another rabbi had said. But when they heard *Yeshua*, they knew that His words were fresh, powerful, and were from God.

"And it came to pass, when Jesus had ended these sayings, the people were astonished at his doctrine: For he taught them as one having authority, and not as the scribes." **Matthew 7:28-29.**

Even the Roman officers were moved by the words of *Yeshua*.

"Then came the officers to the chief priests and Pharisees; and they said unto them, Why have ye not brought him? The officers answered, Never man spake like this man." **John 7:45-46.**

GOD IN HIS MIRACLES

One of the most compelling evidences that *Yeshua* was the God-Man is the miracles that are recorded in the gospels. (Over 35 miracles are recorded) In one sense, we could say that all of the miracles prove His deity. Like the people said in **John 7:31,** *"When Christ cometh, will he do more miracles than these which this man hath done?"* Miracles would vindicate His deity; even *Yeshua* said that if they did not believe in Him, they should believe the miracles that He did. *"Believe me that I am in the Father, and the Father in me: or else believe me for the very works' sake."* **John 14:11.** When John the Baptist, while in prison, began to have doubts about *Yeshua* truly being the Messiah, *Yeshua* sent back to tell John about His miracles:

"Go and shew John again those things which ye do hear and see: The blind receive their sight, and the lame walk, the lepers are cleansed, and the deaf hear, the dead are raised up, and the poor have the gospel preached to them." **Matthew 11:4-5.**

I would like to mention a few miracles that are clear proof that *Yeshua* was truly the God-Man.

"When the ruler of the feast had tasted the water that was made wine; and knew not whence it was: (but the servants which drew the water knew;) the governor of the feast called the bridegroom, And saith unto him, Every man at the beginning doth set forth good wine, and when

men have well drunk, then that which is worse: but thou hast kept the good wine unto now. This beginning of miracles did Jesus in Cana in Galilee, and <u>manifested forth his glory</u>; and his disciples believed on him." **John 2:9-11.**

Notice that *Yeshua* turned the water into wine to manifest forth his glory. No grapes were needed; no sunshine needed, no process of time was needed. He simply had the power to create something from nothing.

"Do ye not yet understand, neither remember the five loaves of the five thousand, and how many baskets ye took up? Neither the seven loaves of the four thousand, and how many baskets ye took up?" **Matt.16:9-10.**

Yeshua created fish and bread to feed thousands on the shore of Galilee. **John 6:1-14, (5,000) Matt.15:32-39, (4,000).** Where did the fish and the bread come from? These miracles that we have heard all of our lives hold a much deeper truth than the average Sunday morning sermon can give. Here is the Man, *Yeshua Ha Notzri*, about thirty years of age, turning clear water into aged wine. He multiplied barley loaves and sardine-sized fish, enough to feed thousands. *Yeshua* saved a bridegroom from being humiliated, and He more than satisfied a hungry multitude. What kind of person could do that? The God-Man!

"Whether is it easier to say to the sick of the palsy, Thy sins be forgiven thee; or to say, Arise, and take up thy bed, and walk? But that ye may know that the Son of man hath power on earth to forgive sins, (he saith to the sick of the palsy,)" **Mark 2:9-10.**

Only the God of the Old Testament could forgive sins, and *Yeshua* could forgive sins when He walked this earth, proving that He was

God in human form. Being two thousand years removed from ancient Israel, we do not understand the magnitude this miracle holds. The people who were there that day could not believe that they had heard a Man say such a thing. *"We never saw it on this fashion."* **Mark 2:12.**

"And Jesus, moved with compassion, put forth his hand, and touched him, and saith unto him, I will; be thou clean. And as soon as he had spoken, immediately the leprosy departed from him, and he was cleansed." **Mark 1:41-42.**

A leper was considered the most unclean in Jewish society, not being allowed to come near a village and if they came close to anybody they had to cry out *"unclean, unclean"*. Anyone who touched a leper was also considered *unclean*. But the scriptures are careful to tell us that *Yeshua* touched the leper, and not only was the leper immediately cleansed, but *Yeshua* remained clean and undefiled. One of the underlying truths in the ministry of *Yeshua*, was the fact that He came in contact with *unclean* people, such as; the demon-possessed, the woman with the issue of blood, raising the dead, lepers, blind, crippled, adulterous women, tax collectors, and Gentiles. *Yeshua* not only showed compassion to them, and healed them, but He also placed them back in society with a *clean* standing. There is only one person who could do that: *Yeshua*, the God-Man!

"And the same day, when the even was come, he saith unto them, Let us pass over unto the other side. And when they had sent away the multitude, they took him even as he was in the ship. And there were also with him other little ships. And there arose a great storm of wind, and the waves beat into the ship, so that it was now full. And he was in the hinder part of the ship, asleep on a pillow: and they awake

him, and say unto him, Master, carest thou not that we perish? And he arose, and rebuked the wind, and said unto the sea, Peace, be still. And the wind ceased, and there was a great calm. And he said unto them, Why are ye so fearful? how is it that ye have no faith? And they feared exceedingly, and said one to another, <u>What manner of man is this</u>, that even the wind and the sea obey him?" **Mark 4: 35-41.**

This passage is filled with many truths, but the primary truth lies in the answer to the question that the disciples asked; *"What manner of man is this, that even the wind and the sea obey him?"* Only the *Elohim* of the Old Testament could speak to the sea and to the wind, and force them to obey him. But in this powerful miracle we see *Yeshua*, as a Man, being able to get into a small ship with His disciples after a very busy day in Capernaum of healing and preaching. They took Him *"even as he was."* We see Him as a Man, asleep in the ship. Then we see that *Yeshua* was more than just a Man, His divinity breaks through and He speaks to a raging storm. It's one thing to perform miracles on humans, but quite another thing to perform miracles on nature.

"And in the fourth watch of the night Jesus went unto them, <u>walking on the sea.</u>" **Matthew 14:25.**

Yeshua proved that He had dominion over nature when He walked on the Sea of Galilee. The same precious feet that had been walking along the dusty roads of Galilee, bringing peace to all, were now walking on top of the waves of the sea, bringing peace to His disciples. It matters not how deep the waters may have been, *Yeshua's* divine power allowed Him to defy the laws of gravity. It was Jewish belief that the sea represented evil, and if that be true, *Yeshua* was also proving that He was stronger than the powers of evil.

"And saith unto them, Go your way into the village over against you: and as soon as ye be entered into it, ye shall find a colt tied, whereon never man sat: loose him, and bring him." **Mark 11:2.**

"And when they had this done, they inclosed a great multitude of fishes: and their net brake." **Luke 5:6.**

"And when he saw a fig tree in the way, he came to it, and found nothing thereon, but leaves only, and said unto it, Let no fruit grow on thee henceforward for ever. And presently the fig tree withered away." **Matt.21:19.**

While walking this earth, *Yeshua* had power over the animal world, the fish world, and could even curse a fig tree just by speaking to it.

"And as he prayed, the fashion of his countenance was altered, and his raiment was white and glistering. And, behold, there talked with him two men, which were Moses and Elias." **Luke 9:30.**

What a strange and mysterious passage of scripture! The humble preacher from Nazareth was concealing His eternal glory. But here, on the Mt. of Transfiguration, His glory burst through and three of the disciples were able to get a glimpse of the future kingdom. What could be more powerful, than Moses and Elijah standing with the very Son of God in glory? As they were discussing His death and resurrection in Jerusalem, *Yeshua* would fulfill what had been written in the law and the prophets concerning His first coming.

"Since the world began was it not heard <u>that any man</u> opened the eyes of one that was born blind." **John 9:32.**

Notice that the scripture here says that no man had ever opened the eyes of one born blind. There were other rabbis who claimed to perform miracles, but no man had ever healed another man that was born blind. But they had never seen a *Man* like *Yeshua*. Many of the rabbis knew that only the Messiah could open the eyes of a blind man, because they knew that the Messiah of Israel would also be God. Certain miracles could only be done by Israel's Messiah! *Yeshua* proved that He was the true Light of the world, and He had come to deliver people out of darkness. This miracle was truly a messianic miracle, and proved that the kingdom age had begun. **Isa.35:5**.

Many of the common people knew that the miracles of *Yeshua* proved that He was the Messiah.

"And many of the people believed on him, and said, When Christ cometh, will he do more miracles than these which this man hath done?" **John 7:31**.

"Jesus said, Take ye away the stone, Martha, the sister of him that was dead, saith unto him, Lord, by this time he stinketh: for he hath been dead four days." **John 11:39**.

Yeshua deliberately waited four days to prove that Lazarus was physically dead. Jews in Bible times did not believe in cremation or embalming. It was Jewish custom that the soul departed the body on the fourth day. *Yeshua* proved that He was the giver of life and that He had power over death. Raising Lazarus from the dead, the daughter of Jairus, **Mark 5:41**, and the widow's son in Nain, **Luke 7:14**, were all prefigures of the resurrection of *Yeshua*.

GOD ON THE CROSS

The birth, the ministry, and the death of the Messiah were all prophesied in the Old Testament. When we study about all of the sin offerings that had to be offered in the history of Israel, we need to keep in mind that they were all pointing to a coming Redeemer who would provide one sacrifice for the sins of the world. We find by reading passages like **Deut.21:23, Psalm 22, Isaiah 53**, and **Zechariah 12**, that the Messiah must die by crucifixion on a tree. It was prophesied hundreds of years even before crucifixion was invented by the Persians, and later used by the Romans. How could the death of one Man take away the sin of the world? It would take a perfect sacrifice in order to satisfy God's holy justice in the universe. The only way this would be possible would be for God to step out of eternity and to become a Man. How could all the sin of the world be laid upon one Man? Humanly speaking, it is impossible. But God's love for humanity sent *Yeshua* supernaturally into the world, in order to do what man could not do. There is one third to one half of the gospel narratives dedicated to the death of *Yeshua*. He came into the world just at the right time, He knew how He was going to die, and He knew when He was going to die. This helps us to better understand why *Yeshua* could not be killed prematurely. This helps us to better understand why His Galilean ministry came to a close when it did, and He took His disciples up to Jerusalem during the feast of Passover. When we travel to Israel each year, being in the Galilee is my favorite place. But I am always reminded that *Yeshua* had to leave the pristine hills and shores of Galilee in order to provide salvation for me. He would come back to Galilee to meet His disciples, but not before He had been nailed to a tree in Jerusalem. Notice these passages, and try to read them in the light of God's foreordained plan.

"From that time forth began Jesus to shew unto his disciples, how that he must go unto Jerusalem, and suffer many things of the elders and chief priests and scribes, and be killed, and be raised the third day." **Matthew 16:21.**

"And it came to pass, when the time was come that he should be received up, he stedfastly set his face to go to Jerusalem." **Luke 9:51.**

"No man taketh it from me, but I lay it down of myself. I have the power to lay it down, and I have power to take it again. This commandment have I received of my Father." **John 10:18.**

"And Jesus answered them, saying, The hour is come, that the Son of man should be glorified. Verily, verily, I say unto you, Except a corn of wheat fall into the ground and die, it abideth alone: but if it die, it bringeth forth much fruit." **John 12:23-24.**

Yeshua had to die being lifted up from the earth. His death could not be from natural causes, He would have to be suspended between heaven and earth. There is something mysteriously magnetic about the cross. Even though the cross was more horrific than we could ever imagine, the love of God through *Yeshua* draws us to salvation.

"And I, if I be lifted up from the earth, will draw all men unto me. This he said, signifying what death he should die." **John 12:32, 33.**

Yeshua came into the world when the religious establishment was so corrupt that they would hate Him. Why? Because *Yeshua* exposed their hypocrisy, and was a threat to their self-righteous way of life. Not all of the religious leaders hated *Yeshua*, but the majority did. This would also fulfill the prophecies that were written in the Psalms.

"But this cometh to pass, that the word might be fulfilled that is written in their law, They hated me without a cause." **Psalm 35:19, 69:4, John 15:25.**

Yeshua came into the world when He knew that His own disciples would be scattered, thus fulfilling another prophecy.

"Then saith Jesus unto them, All ye shall be offended because of me this night: for it is written, I will smite the shepherd, and the sheep of the flock shall be scattered abroad." **Zechariah 13:7, Matthew 26:31.**

When the soldiers gambled over the garments of *Yeshua*, little did they know that this was also fulfilling prophesy.

"And they crucified him, and parted his garments, casting lots: that it might be fulfilled which was spoken by the prophet, They parted my garments among them, and upon my vesture did they cast lots." **Psalm 22:18, Matthew 27:35.**

It was no accident that *Yeshua* was crucified with two other malefactors, this too was prophesied, and that He would show forgiveness to one of them. Jewish history tells us that the thief on the right was named, Dimas, and the thief on the left was named, Gestas.

"And there were also two other, malefactors, led with him to be put to death." **Isaiah 53:12, Luke 23:32.**

"And he said unto Jesus, Lord, remember me when thou comest into thy kingdom. And Jesus said unto him, Verily I say unto thee, to day shalt thou be with me in paradise." **Luke 23:42-32.**

Even the religious leaders and those walking by the cross would mock *Yeshua*. This was all prophesied in the Psalms.

"And they that passed by reviled him, wagging their heads." **Psalm 22:7-8, Matthew 27:39.**

"Likewise the chief priests mocking him, with the scribes and elders, said, He saved others; himself he cannot save. If he be the King of Israel, let him now come down from the cross, and we will believe him. He trusted in God; let him deliver him now, if he will have him: for he said, I am the Son of God." **Psalm 22:8, Matthew 27:41-43.**

When the soldiers came to the three crosses, they broke the legs of both malefactors, but when they came to *Yeshua*, they did not break his legs, because He was already dead. This too was prophesied.

"For these things were done, that the scripture should be fulfilled, a bone of him shall not be broken." **John 19:36.**

Little did the Roman soldiers realize that they too were fulfilling the scriptures, just by looking at the pierced Messiah.

"And again another scripture saith, they shall look on him whom they pierced." **Zechariah 12:10.**

GOD IN HIS RESURRECTION

We know from the scriptures themselves that the resurrection of the Messiah was foretold. Even though it seems more obscure, it is because we do not understand the entire scope of the Old Testament scriptures. How could the Messiah of Israel die at His first coming, and rule and reign on the earth at His second coming, without a resurrection? Just because the Old Testament passage may be referring to something within the history of the nation of Israel, it may also be referring to the first or second coming of Israel's Messiah. Notice a few of the New Testament passages concerning the scriptures and the resurrection of *Yeshua*.

"For as yet they <u>knew not the scripture</u>, that he must rise again from the dead." **John 20:9.**

"For as Jonas was three days and three nights in the whale's belly; so shall the Son of man be three days and three nights in the heart of the earth." **Matthew 12:40.**

"Then he said unto them, O fools, and slow of heart to believe all that the prophets have spoken: Ought not Christ to have suffered these things, and to enter into his glory? And beginning at Moses and all the prophets, he expounded unto them in all the scriptures the things concerning himself." **Luke 24:25-27.**

What scriptures were *Yeshua* referring too? Because of the hidden meanings of the Hebrew language, we cannot know all of the verses that *Yeshua* may have used, but again, try to contemplate on the entire picture of the suffering Messiah and the ruling, reigning Messiah. Here are a few old Hebrew scriptures that *Yeshua* may have used.

"And Abraham said unto his young men, Abide ye here with the ass; and I and the lad will go yonder and worship, and come again to you." **Genesis 22:5.**

"Yet it pleased the Lord to bruise him; he hath put him to grief: when thou shalt make his soul an offering for sin, he shall see his seed, he shall prolong his days, and the pleasure of the Lord shall prosper in his hand." **Isaiah 53:10.**

"For thou wilt not leave my soul in hell; neither wilt thou suffer thine Holy One to see corruption." **Psalm 16:10, Acts 2:27.**

"After two days will he revive us: in the third day he will raise us up, and we shall live in his sight." **Hosea 6:2.**

"For I know that my redeemer liveth, and that he shall stand at the latter day upon the earth." **Job 19:25.**

Yeshua always made mention of His own resurrection when talking about His death. It would take more than just His death to provide eternal life for His people. He would have to go through the pains of death and walk out of the tomb. Again, we must remember that in order for someone to prove that they were the true Messiah of Israel, they had to prove it by the works they did, not by just proclaiming to be the Messiah.

The bodies of the sacrificed animals in the Old Testament had to be brought into the camp, but they had to burned outside the camp. **Hebrews 13:11-12.** Therefore, the Messiah had to be offered up outside the walls of Jerusalem. There are two possible places in Jerusalem where Christians commemorate the death and resurrection of *Yeshua.* One is the Holy Sepulchre, which was on the west side of the temple, and the other is Gordon's Calvary, which lies on the north side. The majority of the Catholics believe that it took place at the Holy Sepulchre's location, while most Protestants claim that it happened at Gordon's Calvary. There is supporting evidence for either place, and both of them were outside the walls of Jerusalem in *Yeshua's* time. One very interesting fact about Gordons' Calvary is that it lies on the north side, and the sin offering was supposed to be on the north side of the altar in **Leviticus 1:11.** It is also interesting that there is a hewn out rock tomb there, that evidently was a rich man's tomb. We know that

Yeshua was not buried in the traditional fashion where there were many other bodies in the same tomb. It was prophesied that the Messiah's grave would be with the rich, and that is what we find in the gospel accounts. **Isa.53:9, Matt.27:57.**

The resurrection of *Yeshua* was not a legend, or a fable, or something that some Jewish scribe invented. It was an historical fact! The fact that *Yeshua* was actually seen after His resurrection proved that He had conquered death and hell, and is the very foundation of the Christian faith. As God, *Yeshua* proved that death could not hold the giver of life!

"And Thomas answered and said unto him, My Lord and my God." **John 20:28.**

When the disciple Thomas saw the crucified and risen *Yeshua*, he declared Him to be the Lord God. Thomas realized that *Yeshua* was God in human form. Try to imagine how galvanized the disciples were to have seen *Yeshua* nailed to a tree, and then to see Him alive after three days?

"Therefore let all the house of Israel know assuredly, that God hath made that same Jesus, whom ye have crucified, both Lord and Christ." **Acts 2:36.**

The resurrection proved that *Yeshua* was truly the Lord and was the long awaited Mashiach of Israel. It was the very same *Yeshua* that the disciples had walked with for over three years. The risen, glorified *Yeshua* would tell the aged apostle John about sixty years later on the Island of Patmos, *"I am he that liveth, and was dead; and behold, I am alive for evermore, amen; and have the keys of hell and death."* **Rev.1:18.** One of the errors of the church over the centuries is that we have the tendency to leave *Yeshua* on the cross, instead of focusing on the living, risen Lord! We need to celebrate the risen *Yeshua* every day, not just on a day we call Easter!

GOD IN HIS ASCENSION

The story of the God-Man *Yeshua* is not complete with His birth, or His ministry, or His death and resurrection. He must be the Lord of heaven! He must finish His work and be exalted in a place of honor and rest! The ascension of *Yeshua* is one of the most underestimated parts of the bible.

"Thou wilt shew me the path of life: in thy presence is fullness of joy; at thy right hand there are pleasures for evermore." **Psalm 16:11.**

"The Lord said unto my Lord, sit thou at my right hand, until I make thine enemies thy footstool." **Psalm 110:1.**

"What and if ye shall see the Son of man ascend up where he was before?" **John 6:62.**

"Then said Jesus unto them, Yet a little while am I with you, and then I go unto him that sent me." **John 7:33.**

"I came forth from the Father, and am come into the world: again, I leave the world, and go to the Father." **John 16:28.**

"Jesus saith unto her, Touch me not; for I am not yet ascended to my Father: but go to my brethren, and say unto them, I ascend unto my Father, and your Father, and to my God, and your God." **John 20:17.**

"And it came to pass, while he blessed them, he was parted from them, and carried up into heaven." **Luke 24:51.**

"And when he had spoken these things, while they beheld, he was taken up; and a cloud received him out of their sight." **Acts 1:9**.

The second coming of *Yeshua* in clouds of glory, presupposes the ascension prior to His return.

"And then shall appear the sign of the Son of man in heaven: and then shall all the tribes of the earth mourn, and they shall see the Son of man coming in the clouds of heaven with power and great glory." **Matthew 24:30.**

YESHUA AS MAN

When I first started traveling to Israel, there I found a great mystery at work inside of my own life. I was blessed with the spiritual aspect of Christ, and yet I was walking on the very same ground where He walked physically. This strange two-fold life of *Yeshua* was at work in my life. I was seeing the very same mountains that *Yeshua* saw, hearing the same water splash on the shore at the Sea of Galilee, experiencing the tremendous heat in the summer months, feeling the western wind in the evening coming off of the Mediterranean Sea, listening to the birds, and seeing the flowers along the hillsides. I could not see my Lord, but I could feel His presence and see the places where He once lived as a Man. I would be teaching about a certain miracle that He performed and try to help the people to see that *Yeshua* was God of very God, and yet, we were standing on the very hallowed ground in which God, who became a Man, performed the miracle. It was a mystery to experience the mundane things of the natural life and at the same time experience the spiritual things of heaven.

As strange as it may sound, it is even stranger for our finite minds to try and grasp the mystery of the God-Man *Yeshua* as we study the scriptures. When we turn the pages of the gospel accounts, we see the mystery unfold and it catches us off guard. Sometimes we see the humanity of *Yeshua,* and we can relate to Him so easily. We think we can feel His poverty, and His compassion for the people, and then, His deity shows up and we have this awesome sense of wonder. All we can do is praise the Lord and rejoice that the very God of heaven came to this earth as one of us! As I have mentioned earlier, the gospels do not attempt to explain to us this mystery, they just set the mystery forth. But the fact that God became a Man in *Yeshua,* we now can see how God thinks, how God feels toward humanity, and He knows everything that we will ever experience in this earthly life.

Even though it is very difficult to know everything about everyday life in *Yeshua's* time, it is very helpful to study about Jewish life during the early part of the first century. This will help us to better understand the lifestyle of *Yeshua* and how He had to deal with the everyday situations. Through his birth, His ministry, and His death, we can see Him being identified with the common people. We know by some of the bones that were found in Galilee, from people who lived during *Yeshua's* time, that He was probably a small to medium stature. We know that He had a beard and His hair was probably down to the shoulders. His skin would have been dark tanned from the sun like everyone else. He walked everywhere that He went, and we know by the accounts in the gospels that the farthest distance north where He walked was Tyre and Sidon, and the farthest south would have been Jerusalem; about 125 miles total. This is not counting His trip to Egypt with His parents after He was born. There certainly were a few aristocrats who followed our Lord, but most of the people were of the common sort.

The historian, Josephus, tells us that there were over 200 towns and villages around the Sea of Galilee. Most of the Jewish families lived together in a community way of life. Most of the towns had a foul odor because of the sewage that was dumped into designated sections in the middle of the streets. The most joyous times of the Jewish people were the Holy Days and Sabbath days. Weddings and funerals would last up to seven days.

During the time of *Yeshua*, the common people of Galilee were just living above existence, mostly sub-existence. About 700,000 Jews lived in Israel, and about 70% of them were called *"am ha eretz"*, *"people of the land"*. The Jews considered that there were only two kinds of people in the world, Jew and Gentile. The Jews worked hard to disassociate themselves with the Gentiles. Try to imagine being controlled by the Romans, who despised the Jewish faith, and then have them to oppress you with heavy taxation. Then they were taxed an additional 15% by the temple priests in Jerusalem. They were taxed well over 50% of what they earned. The synagogues were being controlled by the Pharisees, who were so caught up in the traditions of the rabbis, that they were not leading the people to God. *Yeshua* came into the world during one of the darkest times in the history of Israel. It is said in the scriptures that even Capernaum, the hometown of *Yeshua*, was a place of the *"shadow of death"*. **Matt.4:16.** The fishermen did not have a free market enterprise, like the modern world today. They had to give an account of every fish they caught, and Rome had their tax collectors standing by to collect on every catch. The Galileans were not noted for manufacturing a lot of goods, only the basic needs of the family. It was also a place of terrible disease, as we can see as we read the gospels. The mortality rate was about 50% before they reached the age of five. Malaria, leprosy, demon-possession, and all types of palsy were common among the people. These kinds of people were not employed and were considered people of no value whatsoever to society. The religious people thought that they were cursed of God, and their sins had caused their terrible state. The hot springs around the city of Tiberias provided some temporary ease, but not a permanent cure.

The religious leaders considered the women second class citizens, and they were divorced for trivial reasons. The woman's job was to provide meals for the family, which normally consisted of things like bread, olives, dates, figs, grapes, wine, and sometimes fish. Two meals a day were common among the Jews, breakfast and dinner, while the Romans ate three to four meals a day. Many women turned to prostitution as a way of survival, sense most of them were deprived of education when they were young. The religious people who lived in Jerusalem considered the people of Galilee unlearned and ignorant. It's very interesting that *Yeshua* called these type people to be His closest followers. They were not scarred with the traditions of the religious Jews and He knew that He could make them great for His kingdom. Galilee had been noted for revolts and the start of the Zealot movement began in Gamla of Galilee. Then consider one of the names of *Yeshua* being *"Yeshua of Galilee"*. **Luke 23:6-7.** All of this played into the hands of His betrayal and crucifixion. And yet, our Lord chose to become a Man of the people, in order to know and to feel all that His people were going through. He could have lived in places like Caesarea and surrounded himself with the more prominent people of society. But He came to show His people and to show the world what is really important; that is to know God, and to live the kingdom life. And through His finished work this would be made possible. This would be how every man would be judged in the end. He did not come to set Israel free from the Romans, or to establish some new political movement, but He came to give them a deeper freedom, one that starts from deep inside of their own hearts. His kingdom would defeat the world in a spiritual way.

Let us try to look at some scriptures in the gospel accounts that can help to better understand the humanity of our Lord. Not just for our intellectual thinking, or to think that it all sounds interesting, but so we can better understand our Lord, and walk closer to Him. *Yeshua* knows how it feels to have moments of ecstasy, and to enjoy life at the fullest. He was a Man of joy, who became a Man of sorrows. He wants His children to know that He is always with us, and our pain is His pain. And when death comes, He wants us to know without a doubt, that He has passed through that valley and is waiting for us on the other side. He knows that we are dust. He knows that we fail. He knows our temptations. He knows our tender moments. He knows how it feels to have a broken heart. He knows. He knows. He knows! Oh yes, *Yeshua* was God, but He was also Man!

MAN IN HIS BIRTH

As we mentioned in a previous chapter, the prophecies mentioned in Isaiah said that the Messiah would be *"The Everlasting Father"*, but He would also be a *"child."* **Isa.9:6**. All of the prophecies concerning the birth of the Messiah had to be accomplished through the means of a virgin girl. **Isa.7:14**. *Yeshua* would have to be a child, and would have to be a male child. So we can see the Christmas story unfold with a woman, a man, and a child; Mary, Joseph, and *Yeshua*. What is amazing is the humble way in which He came. In the little village of Bethlehem, in a cave where the animals stayed, and His bed would be a hewn-out rock, feeding trough. *Yeshua* knows what it is like to be rejected even when He came into the world. **Luke 2:7, John 1:11**. He knows what it is like to feel the coldness of a cave, and to have earthly parents who were poor. His first visitors were the lowly shepherds, who were considered unclean by the religious Jews. When one goes underneath the Church of Nativity in Bethlehem today, you get this awesome sense of wonder, trying to fathom the mystery that God would come to such humble circumstances. Bethlehem was a humble village when *Yeshua* was born, maybe no more than five hundred people. The only thing that Mary had to warm the body of *Yeshua* was her own body and swaddling clothes. The moment would have been much more simple and crude than our modern world could ever understand. It would have been quite, the noise of a few animals rustling through the straw, and then, and then, the cry of a newborn babe, it was the Savior of the world! He would cry at His birth and He would cry at His death. A little virgin girl and a humble carpenter from Nazareth would never be the same. The humanity of *Yeshua* really shines through at His birth. The eternal God took upon Himself flesh and bone.

He came into the world during a certain period of time and to a specific place. That is why we find certain world leader's names mentioned and certain places in Israel mentioned in the gospels. Caesar Augustus was the Roman Emperor, and Bethlehem was the place. In order the prophecies to be fulfilled God would orchestrate the historical events of the world. A worldwide census would be taken by Caesar that would send *Yeshua's* earthly parents to the right place. In order to become a Man, God had to use humans for His plan. While Mary nursed the baby *Yeshua*, He was sustaining the universe at the very same time. So we need to connect the incarnation of *Yeshua* with the God of the Old Testament. When we do, we find that the God who created the Jewish people, the God of Abraham, the God of Moses, the God of Elijah, was born as a baby in Israel. He would be a Jew himself, and come through the house and lineage of David just like He said. **II Samuel 7:16.**

"The book of the generation of Jesus Christ, the son of David, the son of Abraham." **Matthew 1:1.**

"And Joseph also went up from Galilee, out of the city of Nazareth, into Judaea, unto the city of David, which is called Bethlehem; (because he was of the house and lineage of David:)" **Luke 2:4.**

"And she brought forth her firstborn son, and wrapped him in swaddling clothes, and laid him in a manger; because there was no room for them in the inn." **Luke 2:7.**

MAN IN HIS CHILDHOOD

The Messiah would grow up in a religious, Jewish family in Nazareth. He humbled himself to be raised in an obscure village like Nazareth. After their return from Egypt, Joseph was given a dream telling him to not settle in Bethlehem, because Herod Archelaus had inherited his father's place in Judaea. They were to go back north to Nazareth, about a three to four days journey. We find him as a twelve year old boy in Jerusalem at the feast of Passover. **Luke 2:42.** *Yeshua* would have known what it was like to run along the hillsides of Nazareth, and to play with family and friends. He would have looked like any other Galilean Jew who lived in Nazareth. Matthew's gospel tells us that He would be called a *"Nazarene"*. **Matt.2:23.** One of the verses that connect Israel's Messiah to being a *Nazarene* is **Isa.11:1;** *"And there shall come forth a rod out of the stem of Jesse, and a Branch (netzer) shall grow out of his roots."* From the very beginning, Joseph and Mary knew that there was something special about *Yeshua.* They didn't understand everything, but certain childhood events would stay in the minds forever.

"And when he was twelve years old, they went up to Jerusalem after the custom of the feast." **Luke 2:42.**

"And he said unto them, How is it that ye sought me? wist ye not that I must be about my Father's business?" **Luke 2:49.**

"And Jesus increased in wisdom and stature, and in favour with God and man." **Luke 2:52.**

From the time *Yeshua* was twelve years old, until the time that He was baptized at thirty years of age, we have nothing recorded. Many have tried to fabricate stories about mysterious miracles that took place during those silent years, but there is no evidence whatsoever. Some scholars say that He worked about three miles away in Zippori, the capital of Galilee, which was being built during his childhood years. It certainly could have happened, but we don't have any proof. We do know that *Yeshua* was a carpenter; in Hebrew, a *"charash"*, which means a *"skilled workman"*. He was probably a worker in stone and wood. He knew what it was like to work hard and to grow weary and tired. *Yeshua* knew what it was like to have brothers and sisters who didn't even believe in Him until after His work on earth was finished. One of His brothers, James, would end up being the first bishop of the church on Mt. Zion, in Jerusalem. Second century Jewish convert Hegesippus, wrote that Jude, the brother of *Yeshua*, had two grandsons, Zoker and James, who were believers during the latter part of the first century.

"Is not this the carpenter, the son of Mary, the brother of James, and Joses, and of Juda, and Simon? are are not his sisters here with us? and they were offended at him. But Jesus said unto them, a prophet is not without honour, but in his own country, and among his own kin, and in his own house." **Mark 6:3-4.**

MAN IN HIS BAPTISM

Yeshua was identified with His people again at His baptism. He would walk some seventy miles down from Nazareth to a place just north of the Dead Sea, where John the Immerser was baptizing. As a Man, He asked John to baptize Him, and John had never seen Him before. But he knew that *Yeshua* was Israel's long awaited Messiah the first time he laid eyes on Him. Try to imagine, being in the middle of a desert wilderness, about twenty miles east of Jerusalem, to the lowest point below sea level on planet earth, two thousand years ago, and the Man *Yeshua* from Nazareth walks into the Jordan River. He is baptized by an Elijah-like preacher, to begin His earthly ministry. John was living in opposition to the priesthood in Jerusalem, by the location of his ministry, by the way he dressed and by his diet. *Yeshua* was placing His approval on John's ministry. No advertisements, no microphones, no newspapers, no television, no cell phones, no electricity, but the Holy Spirit had designed it all for this time and place. It happened in the same area where Joshua had brought the children of Israel across when they first entered the Promised Land. After four hundred long years of not one prophet thundering in Israel, the nation of Israel was not living in idolatry, but they had drifted far from God. Through a radical preacher, God was taking them back to where their forefathers had crossed the Jordan River centuries before. While God was calling Israel to repentance through John, Israel's Messiah would be the One through whom their repentance would be directed too. And yet, He also feels the need to be baptized! As a Man, He was being man's representative. What looked like a very crude, and simple scene in a muddy river, received the applause of heaven. What a sight that must have been!

"Now when all the people were baptized, it came to pass, that Jesus also being baptized, and praying, the heaven was opened, And the Holy Ghost descended in a bodily shape like a dove upon him, and a voice came from heaven, which said, Thou art my beloved son; in thee I am well pleased." **Luke 3:21-22.**

"The next day John seeth Jesus coming unto him, and saith, Behold the Lamb of God, which taketh away the sin of the world." **John 1:29.**

At the beginning of the gospels we see where the forerunner of the Messiah says *"Behold the Lamb of God"*, and the baptism of *Yeshua* was a symbol of His own death, burial, and resurrection. When *Yeshua* was sent to appear before Pontius Pilate, we find these words:

"Then came Jesus forth, wearing the crown of thorns, and the purple robe. And Pilate saith unto them, Behold the man!" **John 19:5.**

The perfect sacrifice for the sin of all the world would be provided by God's Lamb, *Yeshua Ha Mashiach*, and little did Pilate know that the *Man* that was standing in front of him was none other than the very Savior of the world.

MAN IN HIS TEMPTATION

When *Yeshua* entered into the cursed earth, He was entering into Satan's domain. He did not come into the world in some spiritual realm in order to dodge the attacks of Satan, but he came into this world as a Man, in order to defeat Satan and what sin had brought into the world. We have this tremendous moment when *Yeshua* was baptized, with the Father speaking from heaven, and immediately we find these words: *"Then was Jesus led up of the Spirit into the wilderness to be tempted of the devil."* **Matthew 4:1.**

Yeshua could not began His life-changing ministry until He had proven that in His humanity, He could defeat the enemy. He was tempted to turn rocks into bread; to perform miracles to draw attention to Himself, and He was offered the kingdoms of the world. But *Yeshua* refused to turn rocks into bread, but He chose to feed thousands on the shores of Galilee. He chose not to perform miracles to bring attention to Himself but only when the miracles were necessary to reveal His deity, and to help hurting humanity. He chose not the kingdoms of this world, but He came to establish the kingdom of God.

This was not the only time that *Yeshua* would be tempted. The scriptures say that after the temptation, the devil *"departed from him for a season."* **Luke 4:13.** There were many other times when the devil tempted Him through His own earthly family in **John 7:3-5.** The religious leaders were called *"children of the devil"* in **John 8:44.** *Yeshua* was tempted when He was in the Garden of Gethsemane in **Matthew 26:39.** He was tempted finally when He was on the cross to perform a miracle and come down from the cross. **Matthew 27:40.** We must keep in mind that *Yeshua* was under the attack of Satan and the world for centuries before He came. The *"seed of the serpent"* did everything he could to prevent the *"seed of the woman"* from coming into the world. Once Satan realized that he could not stop the Messiah from coming into the world, he did everything he could possibly do to kill him when He was born, to thwart His mission, and to keep him from going to the cross. Because *Yeshua* overcame the wicked one, we have the promise that we too can be more than conquerors through him that loved us. **Romans 8:37.** Again, He understands our temptations, He sympathizes with His people. We have someone to turn too when trials and temptations come. We do not have to yield to that temptation; He will make a way for us to escape.

Hebrews 4:15, I Corinthians 10:13. *Yeshua* not only came to die for our sins, He came to give us life and life more abundantly here and now! **John 10:10.**

MAN IN HIS PRAYERS

"And in the morning rising up a great while before day, he went out, and departed into a solitary place, and there prayed." **Mark 1:35.**

"And it came to pass in those days, that he went out into a mountain to pray, and continued all night in prayer to God." **Luke 6:12.**

"And when he had sent the multitudes away, he went up into a mountain apart to pray: and when the evening was come, he was there alone." **Matthew 14: 23.**

"These words spake Jesus, and lifted up his eyes to heaven, and said, Father, the hour is come, glorify thy son, that they Son also may glorify thee." **John 17:1.**

"I pray for them: I pray not for the world, but for them which thou hast given me; for they are thine." **John 17:9.**

"Neither pray I for these alone, but for them also which shall believe in me through their word." **John 17:20.**

"And he went a little further, and fell on his face, and prayed, saying, O my Father, it if be possible, let this cup pass from me: nevertheless not as I will, but as thou wilt." **Matthew 26:39.**

The prayers of *Yeshua* were given from the mountains of Galilee to the Garden of Gethsemane. As a Man, He felt the need to pray. He was praying for others, that His disciples would understand their mission into the world for the very first time. He prayed as

He was surrendering to do the Father's will, just before they came to arrest Him in the garden. He prayed to the heavenly Father about His finished work that He had been sent to accomplish. He prayed for the security of His disciples and for those who would believe through their word.

There have been times that I wondered if my prayers were heard, because of my lack of faith at the time, but we know that the prayers of *Yeshua* were heard and answered. He even uttered one final prayer when He was on the cross; *"Father, forgive them; for they know not what they do."* **Luke 23:34.** Many of the same people who were responsible for the crucifixion of *Yeshua*, would be saved on the day of Pentecost in **Acts 2**, and **Acts 6:7.**

MAN IN HIS MIRACLES

We must not only see the deity within the miracles that *Yeshua* performed, but also His humanity. While *Yeshua* had power over nature, notice His humanity in these miracles. He falls asleep after a long day of ministry in Capernaum, but gets up and calms the storm. When *Yeshua* walks on the water, He was not twenty feet tall; He was the very same height He was on the land. We have it all happening at a certain time of the night, between three and six in the morning. *Yeshua* is able to put a piece of money in the mouth of the very first fish that comes to Peter's fishing hook, but yet, *Yeshua* mentions the need to pay His own taxes.

"And he was in the hinder part of the ship, asleep on a pillow: and they awake him, and say unto him, Master, carest thou not that we perish?" **Mark 4:38.**

"And in the fourth watch of the night Jesus went unto them, walking on the sea." **Matthew 14:25.**

"Notwithstanding, lest we should offend them, go thou to the sea, and cast an hook, and take up the fish that first cometh up; and when thou hast opened his mouth, thou shalt find a piece of money: that take, and give unto them for me and thee." **Matthew 17:27.**

THE SON OF MAN

The term *"Son of man"* occurs eighty one times in the canonical gospels. It is over one hundred times in the old Hebrew scriptures, with ninety three of them being in the book of Ezekiel. The term normally just meant a human being in Judaism, but it means more when talking about the Messiah. While the terms *"Son of God"* and *"Son of man"* have different meanings, both of them are given to *Yeshua*. The first speaks about His deity, while the second speaks about His humanity. Most Hebrew scholars connect the term *"Son of man"* to the eschatological figure in **Daniel 7:13-14.** In the story of *Yeshua* healing the man born blind in **John 9**, we find this unusual passage:

"Jesus heard that they had cast him out; and when he had found him, he said unto him, Dost thou believe on the Son of God? He answered and said, Who is he, Lord, that I might believe on him? And Jesus said unto him, Thou hast both seen him, and it is he that talketh with thee. And he said, Lord, I believe. And he worshipped him." **John 9:35-38**

Yeshua asked the man if he believed on the *Son of God*, and then told him that the *Son of God* is the one he was listening too and was able to see. Before the *Son of God* could be seen He had to become the *"Son of man"*.

"No man hath seen God at any time; the only begotten Son, which is in the bosom of the Father, he hath declared him." **John 1:18.**

Yeshua even called himself the *"Son of man"* in many passages. When one man evidently had the wrong idea of what it meant to follow *Yeshua*, He told him that being a disciple was not an easy road.

"And Jesus said unto him, Foxes have holes, and birds of the air have nests; but the Son of man hath not where to lay his head."

When the religious leaders said that John the Baptist had a devil because he did not drink or eat, *Yeshua* told them about their inconsistency. As a Man *Yeshua* came, not as John did, but to be among His people and He came eating and drinking, and they rejected Him as their Messiah.

"The Son of man came eating and drinking, and they say, Behold a man gluttonous, and a winebibber, a friend of publicans, and sinners. But wisdom is justified of her children." **Matthew 11:19.**

**He was so human that he grew weary and tired, but yet
he was so divine that he could say, come unto me all ye
that labor and are heavy laden and I will give you rest.
He was so human that he knew what it was like to
be hungry, but he was so divine that he could take
five loaves and two fishes and feed a multitude
He was so human that he knew what it was like to
be thirsty, but he was so divine that he could say, if
any man thirst let him come unto me and drink
He was so human that he felt the need to
pray, but he was so divine that he never had to
confess his sins because he was sinless
He was so human that he fell asleep, but he was so
divine that he arose and calmed a raging storm**

He was so human that he cried, but he was so divine
that he called forth Lazarus from the grave
He was so human that he had to grow in wisdom,
but he was so divine that he holds everything
together by the word of his power
He was so human that he died with a broken heart, but
he was so divine that his death redeemed a lost world
He was so human that his body was laid in a
tomb, but he was so divine that he walked out
of the tomb defeating death and hell

Yeshua referred to himself as the *"Son of man"* when talking about His cross.

"And while they abode in Galilee, Jesus said unto them, the Son of man shall be betrayed into the hands of men: And they shall kill him, and the third day he shall be raised again. And they were exceeding sorry." **Matthew 17:22-23.**

When *Yeshua* talked about His second coming, He used the title the *"Son of man."*

"And then shall they see the Son of man coming in the clouds with great power and glory." **Mark 13:26.**

When *Yeshua* talked about His messianic kingdom to be established on the earth, He used the same title.

"And Jesus said unto them, Verily I say unto you, That ye which have followed me, in the regeneration when the Son of man shall sit in the throne of his glory, ye also shall sit upon twelve thrones, judging the twelve tribes of Israel." **Matthew 19:28.**

When the aged apostle John saw a vision of the glorified Christ, he saw Him still in the form of a Man.

"And in the midst of the seven candlesticks one like unto the Son of man, clothed with a garment down to the foot, and girt about the paps with a golden girdle." **Revelation 1:13.**

MAN ON THE CROSS

"Forasmuch then as the children are partakers of flesh and blood, he also himself likewise took part of the same; that through death he might destroy him that had the power of death, that is, the devil." **Hebrews 2:14.**

The primary reason for *Yeshua* coming into this world was to die on the cross and to defeat death and hell. God is the Eternal Spirit and He cannot die, so by the incarnation God could be capable of physical death. Even though our minds cannot grasp the full understanding behind the cross, there are several things we must remember.

1) *God's holy justice had to be met*
2) *The holy scriptures had to be fulfilled*
3) *Yeshua's blood would provide righteousness for His people*
4) *Eternal life had to be secured for God's people*
5) *Satan had to be defeated*

So as a Man, *Yeshua's* mission was not to just be an example for His people to follow. He didn't come just to give us some good sermons and to tell us how we are to live. He came to provide salvation for His people. Remember, that *Yeshua* means *"Yahweh saves"*. So when the hour had come, the Man *Yeshua* was arrested in the Garden of Gethsemane, taken to the house of Caiaphas, sent to Pontius Pilate, who sent Him to Herod Antipas, then back to Pilate. We see them beating the Man *Yeshua*, placing a crown of thorns upon His head, and delivering Him to be crucified. *Yeshua* would have been led through the streets of Jerusalem, to outside the walls, to a place called in the Hebrew tongue, *Golgotha*, and in the Latin tongue, *Calvary*. **John 19:17, Luke 23:33.** We believe that the Man *Yeshua* was crucified on the side of a major road leading out of Jerusalem, relatively low to the ground, so the people could walk by and laugh and jeer, and also to prevent anyone who would ever consider going against Rome. It was not Roman tradition to crucify people on top of hills but along the busy highways.

While on the cross, the Man *Yeshua* spoke to His mother, *"Behold thy son"*, and then spoke to His apostle John, *"Behold thy mother."* **John 19:26-27.** He would cry, *"Eli, Eli, lama sabachthani, that is to say, My God, my God, why hast thou forsaken me?"* **Matthew 27:46.** While hanging on the tree, *Yeshua* said *"Father, forgive them; for they know not what they do"*. **Luke 23:34.** He spoke to the one of the thieves hanging next to Him, *"Verily I say unto thee, To day shalt thou be with me in paradise"*. **Luke 23:43.** The Man *Yeshua* cried, *"I Thirst,"* just before He said, *"It is finished"*. **John 19:30.** He finally cried with a loud voice, and *"yielded up the ghost"*. **Matthew 27:50.**

"But one of the soldiers with a spear pierced his side, and forthwith came there out blood and water." **John 19:34.**

The scars that were made by the Romans on the body of the Lord *Yeshua* will remain throughout all of eternity.

MAN IN THE TOMB

"And after this Joseph of Arimathaea, being a disciple of Jesus, but secretly for fear of the Jews, besought Pilate that he might take away the body of Jesus: and Pilate gave him leave. He came therefore, and took the body of Jesus. And there came also Nicodemus, which at first came to Jesus by night, and brought a mixture of myrrh and aloes, about and hundred pound weight. Then took they the body of Jesus, and wound it in linen clothes with the spices, as the manner of the Jews is to bury. Now in the place where he was crucified there was a garden; and in the garden a new sepulchre, wherein was never man yet laid. There laid they Jesus therefore because of the Jews' preparation day; for the sepulchre was nigh at hand." **John 19:38-42.**

It was divinely ordained for Pilate to give up the body of *Yeshua* to Joseph of Arimathaea. It was not the Roman custom to give the body away to any family members. They normally would take the bodies that had been crucified and throw them in a mass grave and burn them. But the prophet Isaiah had said that the body of the Messiah would be buried in a grave. **Isa.53:9.** Joseph was one of the religious leaders, along with Nicodemus, who did believe in *Yeshua*, but kept it secret until now. **John 12:42.** We know by the scriptures telling us that Nicodemus was the one *"which at the first came to Jesus by night"*, that the conversation that he had with *Yeshua* back in **John 3**, forever changed his life. No doubt, when Nicodemus saw *Yeshua* lifted up on the cross, it brought back to his mind what *Yeshua* had told him **John 3:14.** It's interesting that the religious man Nicodemus, who once only understood about the law of Moses, was being turned into a man of the Spirit. Notice that the term *"body of Jesus"* is mentioned several times in this passage of scripture. His body had been prepared, **Hebrews 10:5,** to be the perfect sacrifice for the sins of the whole world. I

John 2:2. After all the sins of the world were laid upon the body of *Yeshua*, **I Peter 2:24**, God had ordained two men to take His body down from the cross and place it in a special tomb, *"wherein was never man yet laid"*.

MAN IN HIS RESURRECTION

The woman, Mary Magdalene, was chosen to be the first one to see the Man *Yeshua* after He had risen from the dead. She became the *"apostle to the apostles."* The one who had set her free from demonic possession, and who had included her among His closest followers, was the same Lord that she would see after He had conquered death and the grave. He would even call her by her name.

"Jesus saith unto her, Mary." **John 20:16.**

"Mary Magdalene came and told the disciples that she had seen the Lord, and that he had spoken these things unto her." **John 20:18.**

1) She would see the risen Lord face to face
2) She would hear the voice of the risen Messiah
3) She would go and tell the men disciples

Yeshua died as a Man, He was buried as a Man, and He arose as a Man. He proved it to His disciples by shewing them His hands and His side. Another way that *Yeshua* proved to His disciples that He was risen in bodily form, was by eating and drinking in front of them. This was a Jewish way of proving physical life.

"Then the same day at evening, being the first day of the week, when the doors were shut where the disciples were assembled for fear of the Jews, came Jesus and stood in the midst, and saith unto them, Peace

be unto you. And when he had so said, he shewed unto them his hands and his side. Then were the disciples glad, when they saw the Lord.”

“And it came to pass, as he sat at meat with them, he took bread, and blessed it, and brake, and gave to them. And their eyes were opened, and they knew him; and he vanished out of their sight.” **Luke 24:30-31.**

“Behold my hands and my feet, that it is I myself: handle me, and see; for a spirit hath not flesh and bones, as ye see me have. And when he had this spoken, he shewed them his hands and his feet. And while they yet believed not for joy, and wondered, he said unto them, Have ye here any meat? And they gave him a piece of broiled fish, and of an honeycomb. And he took it, and did eat before them.” **Luke 24:39-43.**

“Jesus saith unto them, Come and dine. And none of the disciples durst ask him, Who art thou? Knowing that it was the Lord. Jesus then cometh, and taketh bread, and giveth them, and fish likewise. This is now the third time that Jesus shewed himself to his disciples, after that he was risen from the dead.” **John 21:12-14.**

“To whom also he shewed himself alive after his passion by many infallible proofs, being seen of them forty days, and speaking of the things pertaining to the kingdom of God.” **Acts 1:3.**

“........whom they slew and hanged on a tree: Him God raised up the third day, and shewed him openly; Not to all the people, but unto witnesses chosen before of God, even to us, who did eat and drink with him after he rose from the dead.” **Acts 10:39-41.**

The risen Christ stands at the very heart of the Christian faith. The fact that the Man *Yeshua* walked out of the tomb, is the reason the gospel conquered the world empires. Just a faith in someone who died for a just cause would not last. Just a faith in someone who performed miracles and brought powerful sermons would not last. But when *Yeshua* died on the cross, and was buried, and then came forth from the grave as the God-Man; that conquered the world! Listen to these powerful words that were written by the apostle Paul about thirty years later.

"For I delivered unto you first of all that which I also received, how that Christ died for our sins according to the scriptures; And that he was buried, and that he rose again the third day according to the scriptures: And that he was seen of Cephas, then of the twelve: After that, he was seen of above five hundred brethren at once; of whom the greater part remain unto this present, but some are fallen asleep. After that, he was seen of James; then of all the apostles. And last of all he was seen of me also, as of one born out of due time." **I Corinthians 15:3-8.**

"And if Christ be not risen, then is our preaching vain, and your faith is also vain. Yea, and we are found false witnesses of God; because we have testified of God that he raised up Christ: whom he raised not up, if so be that the dead rise not. For if the dead rise not, then is not Christ raised: And if Christ be not raised, your faith is vain; ye are yet in your sins. Then they also which are fallen asleep in Christ are perished. If in this life only we have hope in Christ, we are of all men most miserable." **I Corinthians 15:14-19.**

"For since by man came death, by man came also the resurrection of the dead." "For as in Adam all die, even so in Christ shall all be made alive." **I Corinthians 15:21-22.**

It was a man who allowed sin to come into the world, and it was a Man who died for the sins of the world. Because of one man's sin, everyone has to die, but because of one Man's resurrection, we can live forever! It is the power of the risen *Yeshua* that enables us to live the Christian life.

"But if the Spirit of him that raised up Jesus from the dead dwell in you, he that raised up Christ from the dead shall also quicken your mortal bodies by His spirit that dwelleth in you." **Romans 8:11.**

The power of the resurrection never ends. Every time someone surrenders their life to *Yeshua,* and believes in His death and resurrection, the story starts all over again.

"That if thou shalt confess with thy mouth the Lord Jesus, and shalt believe in thine heart that God hath raised him from the dead, thou shalt be saved." **Romans 10:9.**

MAN IN HIS ASCENSION

When *Yeshua* was about to depart into heaven, He took them over the Mt. of Olives, to the little village of Bethany. One last time He showed them His pierced hands. In the law of Moses, if a priest had any blemish in his hands he could not minister. **Lev.21:16-23.** One of the prevailing thoughts was, if a priest had any kind of blemish, when he gave the blessing the people would be distracted from the blessing. The Messiah *Yeshua* gave a final blessing to His disciples with nail-scarred hands. The prints in His hands were part of the blessing!

"And he led them out as far as to Bethany, and he lifted up his hands, and blessed them." **Luke 24:50.**

The disciples had walked with *Yeshua* for over three years, and they had experienced so many life-changing moments. He had been their life and their joy. Through doubts and fears, He was molding them into powerful disciples who would take the gospel into the world for the very first time. Even though they did not understand His mission at His first coming, He would explain the scriptures to them after the resurrection that He must suffer first and then return in clouds of glory. **Luke 24:26, 44.**

There was a thought among some of the rabbis that there would be two Messiahs. One Messiah would be *Yeshua Ben Joseph*, who would suffer for the sins of His people. The other Messiah would be *Yeshua Ben David*, who would rule and reign from Jerusalem. As *Yeshua* was ascending back to heaven, He wanted them to know that when He returns, He will be the very same Lord. There's only one Messiah! He will come back to the very same Mt. of Olives that He ascended from.

"And while they looked stedfastly toward heaven as he went up, behold, two men stood by them in white apparel; Which also said, Ye men of Galilee, why stand ye gazing up into heaven? this same Jesus, which is taken up from you into heaven, shall so come in like manner as ye have seen him go into heaven." **Acts 1:10-11.**

And even though we have never seen our Lord face to face, we love Him, and we know that one day we will see Him and will be made just like Him.

"Jesus saith unto him, Thomas, because thou hast seen me, thou hast believed: blessed are they that have not seen, and yet have believed." **John 20:29.**

"Beloved, now are we the sons of God, and it doth not yet appear what we shall be: but we know that, when he shall appear, we shall be like him; for we shall see him as he is." **I John 3:2.**

MAN IN HIS RETURN

Without belaboring the point, I want to mention a few passages regarding the second coming of the Man *Yeshua*. The sacred scriptures record for us that He is coming back to this earth in the form of a Man! When I read this passage it brings tears to my eyes, knowing that one day all of the saved will be in the army of the Lord. No one can predict when He is going to return, but we know that history will come to an end as we know it. One day all of the world will know truly that *Yeshua* is the Lord God Almighty!

"And I saw heaven opened, and behold a white horse; and he that sat upon him was called Faithful and True, and in righteousness he doth judge and make war. His eyes were as a flame of fire, and on his head were many crowns; and he had a name written, that no man knew, but he himself. And he was clothed with a vesture dipped in blood: and his name is called The Word of God. And the armies which were in heaven followed him upon white horses, clothed in fine linen, white and clean. And out of his mouth goeth a sharp sword, that with it he should smite the nations: and he shall rule them with a rod of iron: and he treadeth the winepress of the fierceness and wrath of Almighty God. And he hath on his vesture and on his thigh a name written, KING OF KINGS, AND LORD OF LORDS." **Revelation 19:11-16.**

We will look at this powerful passage again in the next chapter, but notice the different titles that are given to Yeshua: "Faithful and True," "The Word of God," "Almighty God," and "KING OF KINGS, AND LORD OF LORDS." One of the great prophetic books in the bible is the book of Zechariah. The Lord spoke through him describing many of the events regarding Israel when their Messiah returns. It will be a national Day of Atonement when Israel sees the pierced hands of their Messiah. Notice also the personal pronouns *"me"* and *"I"* in these verses. This is showing that the One who was speaking through Zechariah was the Messiah, *Yeshua,* Himself!

"And I will pour upon the house of David, and upon the inhabitants of Jerusalem, the spirit of grace and of supplications: and they shall look upon <u>me</u> whom they have pierced, and they shall mourn for him, as one mourneth for his only son, and shall be in bitterness for him, as one that is in bitterness for his firstborn." **Zechariah 12:10.**

"And one shall say unto him, What are these wounds in thine hands? Then he shall answer, Those with which <u>I</u> was wounded in the house of my friends." **Zechariah 13:6.**

The prophet also describes the coming Messiah as a Man, when He plants His feet on the Mt. of Olives.

"And his feet shall stand in that day upon the Mount of Olives, which is before Jerusalem on the east, and the mount of Olives shall cleave in the midst thereof toward the east and toward the west, and there shall be a very great valley; and half of the mountain shall remove toward the north, and half of it toward the south." **Zechariah 14:4.**

FINAL THOUGHTS

There are several times in the scriptures where God and *Yeshua* are mentioned as being co-equal.

SAVIOR

"For I am the <u>Lord</u> **(Yehovah)** *<u>thy God</u>* **(Elohim)**, *the Holy One of Israel, <u>thy Saviour</u>."* **Isaiah 43:3a.**

"For unto you is born this day in the city of David a Saviour, which is Christ the Lord." **Luke 2:11.**

"Looking for that blessed hope, and the glorious appearing of the great <u>God</u> and our <u>Saviour Jesus Christ</u>." **Titus 2:13.** (Notice the conjunction "and")

"Grace and peace be multiplied unto you through the knowledge of God, and of Jesus our Lord." **II Peter 2:2.**

THE LORD

"The voice of him that crieth in the wilderness, Prepare ye the way of the Lord, **(Yehovah)** *make straight in the desert a highway for our God* **(Elohim)**."* **Isaiah 40:3.**

"For this is he that was spoken of by the prophet Esaias, saying, The voice of one crying the in the wilderness, Prepare ye the way of the Lord, make his paths straight." **Matthew 3:3.** (Isaiah was speaking of John the Baptist who prepared the way for *Yehovah, Elohim,* or *Yeshua*)

KING OF KINGS AND LORD OF LORDS

"I have trodden the winepress alone; and the people there was none with me: for I will tread them in mine anger, and trample them in my fury; and their blood shall be sprinkled upon my garments, and I will stain all my raiment. For the day of vengeance is in mine heart, and the year of my redeemed is come." **Isaiah 63:3-4.**

"Then shall the Lord **(Yehovah)** *go forth, and fight against those nations, as when he fought in the day of battle."* **Zechariah 14:3.**

"And I saw heaven opened, and behold a white horse; and he that sat upon him was called Faithful and True **(Yeshua in Rev.3:7),** *and in righteousness <u>he doth judge and make war</u>. His eyes were as a flame of fire, and on his head were many crowns; and he had a name written, that no man knew, but he himself. And he was clothed with <u>a vesture</u> <u>dipped in blood</u>: and his name is called the Word of God. And the armies which were in heaven followed him upon white horses, clothed in fine linen, white and clean. And out of his mouth goeth a sharp sword, that with it he should smite the nations: and he shall rule them with a rod of iron: and he <u>treadeth the winepress</u> of the fierceness and wrath of Almighty God. And he hath on his vesture and on his thigh a name written, KING OF KINGS, AND LORD OF LORDS."* **Rev.19:11-16**

"That thou keep his commandment without spot, unrebukeable, until the appearing of our Lord Jesus Christ: Which in his times he shall

shew, who is the blessed and only Potentate, the King of kings, and Lord of lords." **I Timothy 6:14-15.**

The God of the Prophets is called by the same title as the *Yeshua* of the book of the Revelation.

"Thus saith the Lord the King of Israel, and his redeemer the Lord of hosts; I am the first, and I am the last; and beside me there is no God." **Isaiah 44:6.**

"I am Alpha and Omega, the beginning and the end, the first and the last." **Rev.22:13.**

The very first verse in the sacred scriptures starts with *"God"*, and the very last verse in the sacred scriptures ends with *"Lord Jesus Christ."*

"In the beginning God created the heaven and the earth." **Gen.1:1**

"The grace of our Lord Jesus Christ be with you all. Amen." **Rev.22:21.**

 *(The Messianic grafted-in symbol was found in one cave on top of Mt. Zion, in Jerusalem. The cave is where first century Jewish Christians met to worship during the time of persecution, possibly after the stoning of Stephen. The symbol depicts a major turning point in the history of Christianity. Peter had preached to the Gentile Cornelius in Caesarea, in Acts 10, and for the first time, officially, a Gentile could receive the Holy Spirit without having to keep the Law of Moses. This caused a division at the first church in Jerusalem, where James, the half brother of Yeshua, was the first Bishop. James stood up in Acts 15 and made it clear that the Gentiles did not have to adhere to the Law of Moses, and that God was calling out a people for His name. Acts 15:14. This symbol shows that Gentile believers are grafted-in to Israel, Rom.11:17. The Menorah is the symbol of Israel, and the Messiah was the Seed of Abraham, and the Star of David shows that the Messiah was also the Son of David. The upside down fish became an early symbol of the believers in Yeshua)*

CPSIA information can be obtained at www.ICGtesting.com
Printed in the USA
LVOW11s0351040915

452738LV00001B/1/P